How to Have a Great Retirement on a Limited Budget

Diane
Warner

How to Have a Great Retirement on a Limited Budget

Diane
Warner

Writer's
Digest
Books

Cincinnati, Ohio

How to Have a Great Retirement on a Limited Budget. Copyright © 1992 by
Diane Warner. Printed and bound in the United States of America. All rights reserved.
No part of this book may be reproduced in any form or by any electronic or mechanical
means including information storage and retrieval systems without permission in
writing from the publisher, except by a reviewer, who may quote brief passages in a
review. Published by Writer's Digest Books, an imprint of F&W Publications, Inc., 1507
Dana Avenue, Cincinnati, Ohio, 45207; 1(800)289-0963. First edition.

96   95   94   93   92   5   4   3   2   1

Library of Congress Cataloging-in-Publication Data

Warner, Diane
    How to have a great retirement on a limited budget / Diane Warner. — 1st ed.
        p.   cm.
    Includes bibliographical references and index.
    ISBN 0-89879-509-5 (pbk.)
    1. Retirement—United States—Planning. 2. Retirees—United States—Life skills
guides. I. Title.
HQ1063.2.U6W37   1992
646.7'9—dc20   91-43153
                                                                                CIP

Edited by Mark Garvey
Designed by Paul Neff

To my Mom.
Thanks for your
love and
encouragement.

Acknowledgments

I want to thank the retirees all over the country who completed the research questionnaires and agreed to be interviewed.

Thanks to the staffs of Pine Lakes Country Club in North Fort Myers, Florida; Sun City Tucson in Tucson, Arizona; and Bristol Village in Waverly, Ohio. Special thanks to Tony Wise, Dianne Weichert, Kathryn Griffin, Rod Young, Lou England and Henrietta Terrazas. I also appreciate the help of the staffs of Stanislaus County Library in Modesto and Turlock, California, and my English-teacher daughter, Lynn.

Thanks, too, to my editor Mark Garvey for your creative ideas and encouragement.

Table of Contents

Introduction

Congratulations! You're finally retiring—that long-dreamed-of event when you'll leave the work force and enter a life of leisure. Ah, the bliss of sleeping in, reading the *entire* morning paper for a change, and puttering for hours at your workbench. Or, perhaps you'll rendezvous at the clubhouse before a delicious round of golf. Of course, you'll no longer need a calculator to add up your golf score for you'll now have plenty of time to sharpen your game. Why, you might even build that putting green in the backyard, the one you've been picturing for years! Your poor buddies are back on the job, punching the clock, counting the years until they too can break away from that dictator called "work."

What? You do have *one* worry? How are you going to get by on only seventy percent of the income you've been used to receiving? (That is the average most couples will get when they retire. And you may not have prepared for retirement as you should.) Do you remember hearing the experts say you should have saved 10 percent of your income toward retirement throughout your working life?

Most couples never did save and invest as they intended. You know. There was the car accident, the double wedding, and the two children in grad school who needed help from Mom and Dad. Who had time to think about rolling over anything but the family dog because you were looking for your lost slipper? Besides, there would be plenty of time to think about saving later on, right?

Whoops! Who would've guessed you would receive the "golden handshake," that questionable honor offered to so many middle-aged workers? This handshake is given to a worker who hasn't quite reached retirement age in exchange for certain incentives, usually cash payoffs. The cash payoff becomes enticing because the worker can retire at a much earlier age than expected, get away from a job that has become dull and tedious, and begin a life of leisure. The worker congratulates himself on still feeling good enough to enjoy the things he used to have to cram into his yearly vacation. It's no wonder most workers gladly take the golden handshake. In fact, more than 60 percent of us retire before age sixty-five.

Whether you took that "golden handshake," or otherwise found yourself unprepared for retirement, you may be experiencing "retirement shock." This shock hits many retired couples, and instead of experiencing joy and euphoria, they slide into a depressive funk because they aren't prepared financially, in spite of any onetime cash payoff they may have received.

If you're retiring before age fifty-nine and a half, you can't draw on your IRA or Keogh, if you have one. You can't begin receiving Social Security benefits until you turn sixty-two. Should you look for another job? If so, how will you survive if you must take one that pays less than your present income?

That's where this book comes in. It's written to encourage you and help you live a quality retirement, even though your income may be low. You'll find great comfort within these pages, for you'll hear about actual retired couples and their actual retirement budgets. You'll find that retired couples all over the country are living well on less retirement income than you may have. I have interviewed these couples and discovered their secrets. In every budget category you *will* find ways to have a *quality* retirement well within your expected income.

I wrote my last book, *How to Have a Big Wedding on a Small Budget*, out of the frustration of planning a large wedding for our daughter on a very small budget. Through research and ingenuity we were able to give our daughter a $13,000 wedding for under $3,500. And that book is showing others how they can do it too, and on even smaller budgets than that!

This retirement book evolved in much the same way. I'm fifty-three and my husband is fifty-five. We plan an early retirement, but are caught in the same financial dilemma as many of you. The logical solution to some of us may be to wait until we are as close to sixty-five as possible, giving

us more time to save that nest egg. However, many of us don't want to wait that long. Therefore, the research I've done for this book, including the interviews with many retired couples, will help all of us plan a manageable retirement budget, so we can live comfortably within our income.

You'll discover all kinds of ways to save money during your retirement years *without sacrificing the quality* of this exciting time. After all, if you retire at fifty-five, for example, you're still expecting to live another third of your life, and there's no reason why it can't be the best third of all! By the way, one-quarter of the population of the United States—sixty million people—are over fifty years old.

If you've already been living on a meager budget and don't expect that to change in retirement, you may say to yourself, "What's new?" But, this isn't true. I'll show you how to save money and make your meager budget stretch to the point where you will actually feel like you've had a raise. You'll see!

After reading this book, you'll find that it's all a matter of prioritizing your spending. Your retirement life-style (housing, leisure activities, entertainment, travel) will all come down to this: Make smart choices! You'll see what I mean as we go along, but you must realize that only *you* can make the choices that will determine the quality of your life during the remaining years.

If you are now retired on a much smaller income than you ever imagined, it may be more difficult to change your spending habits, but you *can do it*! My challenge is to help you learn ways to save and stretch, by substituting and eliminating, without sacrificing on the quality you love. If you are an avid golfer, for example, there *is* such a thing as a public golf course. And it can be just as much fun. You might even like it better than the expensive country club! Many of you will be introduced to ideas that seem novel, but changing your life means opening your mind.

Meanwhile, if the idea of retirement, especially on small budget, is "stressing you out," just remember that this stress is quite normal. The Metropolitan Life Insurance Company did a study that shows that even *good* things cause stress. And, I hope you consider retirement a good thing!

Keep your chin up! After reading this book, I hope you'll feel greatly encouraged. No "retirement shock" for you! Your retirement *will* be the satisfying, euphoric time you've always dreamed about, and I want to have a small part in your success!

Chapter One

The Biggest Bang for the Buck

[Retirement Locales and Life-styles]

"I just want to be near our kids and grandchildren. I know this means we'll have to stay in this high-cost area, but we cut down in other ways." This was the comment of a retired couple who lives in San Mateo, California, a very expensive city in which to live. Because their retirement income is below average, they must sacrifice to be close to family. They rarely travel or go out to eat, their only car is ten years old, and they live in a one-bedroom apartment, but they think the sacrifices are worth it.

Another couple states: "All we want to do is travel, so we bought the best RV we could afford and most of our money goes into it. That's why our main residence is a small mobile home we paid cash for." This retired couple obviously doesn't mind this type of home base so long as they can have their recreational vehicle. Both of them worked right up to retirement and were frustrated because they could only squeeze in three weeks of RVing each year. They always said that when they re-

One-quarter of the population of the United States is over fifty years old.

tired they wanted to be able to travel, and by paying cash for a small mobile home, they're able to do it.

I interviewed another couple who lives in a retirement village that offers golf, tennis, spa, etc. Because they chose to retire in Florida, a comparatively inexpensive state in which to live, they manage extremely well on a meager retirement budget. In Chapter Thirteen we'll go over their finances in detail, along with the budgets of other retirees.

Couple number four are "stay-at-homes." They still live in the house where they raised their family, and their dream is to stay there. They just want to putter in the yard, watch television, work on crafts, and occasionally have friends over for a barbecue.

Each of these four couples has a different life-style, and your choice of a retirement life-style, of course, determines your retirement budget. The couple who chose to RV it have a housing budget of only $250 a month, but their "Travel and Entertainment" funds take the biggest chunk of their monthly income. They add to their travel fund, too, by robbing as much as possible from their gasoline, food and ''hobby'' allowances since they're rarely home anyway. What a life-style! Sounds good to me. I'll bet they rarely cook for company or worry over high utility bills. I interviewed another RV-ing couple who has a plaque mounted on the back of their Winnebago that reads:

We're Retired: No Telephone, No Alarm Clock, No Doorbell, No Money.

There is a lot of truth to that plaque if a couple tries to maintain a big family home while they're RVing it all over the country. If a couple wants this type of life-style and are on a tight retirement budget, they'll almost certainly need to cut down on their home base expenses.

Because couple number four has decided to hang onto their family homestead, which can be an expensive decision, they have a budget lopsided in just the opposite way. Their housing, utilities, home taxes, insurance, ''hobby'' and food allowances eat up a high percentage of their income. They don't allot a dime toward travel. They both traveled for years on their jobs and longed for the day when they could enjoy their home. While the golfing couple is buying new clubs, couple number four is buying petunias to plant by the front gate.

Every retiree is different. What kind of life-style do you want? Statistics show that 86 percent of retired couples in America choose to stay around the area where they worked. Because they want to be near family and friends, or just because they love the familiarity of their hometown, they decide to pursue their life-style within this safe environment. I was surprised that only 14 percent of retired couples move to other states or areas within their home state. After all, entire books are written pointing out the pros and cons of retiring in various areas of the U.S. These statistics tell which are the best retirement areas based on cost of living, types and costs of housing, climate, health care services, the availability of part-time jobs for retired people, leisure and recreational opportunities, lowest taxes, and numbers of other interesting criteria.

Because we're mainly interested in those factors pertaining to our pocketbooks, let's examine a few. First, according to *Retirement Places Rated*, by David Savageau, these are the top cities that make a tight retirement budget easier to survive:

- *Fayetteville, Arkansas*
- *Harrison, Arkansas*
- *Benton County, Arkansas*
- *Grand Lake, Oklahoma*
- *Athens, Texas*
- *Paris, Tennessee*
- *Brownsville, Texas*
- *Kerrville, Texas*
- *Murray, Kentucky*

Taking only housing into account, including utilities, taxes and all monthly costs, these states are said to have the most reasonable retirement housing:

• *Arizona*	• *Michigan*
• *Texas*	• *Kentucky*
• *Oklahoma*	• *Missouri*

- *Florida*
- *Georgia*
- *Utah*
- *Montana*

Obviously, there aren't enough pages to describe every option in detail, but I can pass on some excellent research that covers your alternatives and what they'll cost. We'll delve into the specifics in later chapters, but perhaps this general information will stimulate your creative juices and get you excited about your choices. Let's face it, by the time we're our age, we've become quite comfortable in our ruts, but it may be time to lift our heads and see what's out there.

We'll get into retirement housing costs very specifically in the next chapter. If you already live in one of these states, great! Otherwise, it's up to each couple to decide whether they want to become part of the 14 percent that makes "the big move" for the sake of their budget.

In Chapter Seven, we'll cover the tax aspects of our retirement budgets, but you should be aware that Alaska, Florida, Nevada, South Dakota, Tennessee, Texas, Washington and Wyoming have *no personal income tax*. Just another thing to consider when selecting a locale to accompany your new life-style.

How about part-time jobs for retired people? Did you know that if you need to pad your income with a part-time job for a few years, the worst place to live is a college town? They're glutted with hungry college students, looking for any type of work they can get. This is fierce competition for a retired person to fight. In Chapters Eleven and Twelve, we'll find dozens of ways to make ends meet during these lean retirement years, but while we're talking about retirement locales, these happen to be some of the best locations for obtaining part-time work:

- *Orlando, Florida*
- *Phoenix, Arizona*
- *West Palm Beach, Florida*
- *Hollywood, Florida*
- *San Diego, California*
- *Austin, Texas*
- *Las Vegas, Nevada*
- *Miami, Florida*
- *Fort Myers, Florida*
- *San Antonio, Texas*
- *Portsmouth, New Hampshire*
- *Myrtle Beach, South Carolina*
- *Carson City, Nevada*
- *Salinas, California*
- *Colorado Springs, Colorado*

> *Tucson, Arizona, has more than 360 days of sunshine each year.*

According to a study showing which retirement locales have had the highest increases in population growth from 1985 to 1990, eight of the top twenty are located in Florida. This is no surprise since Florida boasts the second highest population of people over sixty-five in the country. The only state with a higher percentage is Rhode Island, whose senior citizens don't seem to want to move out of their state. Florida, on the other hand, has the most retirees moving *in* from other states.

As I researched this book, I visited as

many retirement communities as possible so I could give you my up-close-and-personal assessment of their claims. A "must" on my list of places to visit is Florida's Fort Myers-Cape Coral-Sanibel Island area. It was ranked as the best overall place to retire in *Retirement Places Rated*. This ranking is based on seven criteria: money matters, housing, climate, personal safety, services, working and leisure living.

I spent a week in this area, and I can certainly see why retirees flock there and love it. The gulf breezes keep heat and humidity bearable, shopping and services abound, and those perfect white sand beaches are breathtaking. Just thirty miles north of Naples — the pricey area that boasts more millionaires than any other city in the country — the Fort Myers area is affordable and has many of the same advantages.

Another community I made a point to visit is Sun City Tucson. I found the desert there to be uniquely beautiful, and the residents seemed serene with their choice of retirement life-style.

Whether you love tennis or swimming, the ocean or the mountains, lake-fishing or horseback riding, a community is out there for you. I recommend you write the chambers of commerce for the cities and states of most interest. They have directories of communities in their areas and can put you in contact with where to send for information, which will usually come in

Eight of the country's ten fastest growing communities are in southern Florida.

color brochures explaining amenities. If several of the communities sound especially interesting, be sure to visit them personally before making a decision. If at all possible, never make a retirement move without physically inspecting the premises. In fact, stay a few days if you can; get a feel for it. Talk to other retirees living there before making your decision.

You'll probably want to check out the entire Sun Belt, which is not only drawing retirees, but the U.S. population as a whole. By the Sun Belt I mean these states in the south and west: North Carolina, South Carolina, Georgia, Florida, Alabama, Mississippi, Louisiana, Arkansas, Texas, New Mexico, Arizona, Southern California and Hawaii. In addition to the Sun Belt there are hundreds of other pockets of retirees tucked here and there. Look for ideas in the back of *Modern Maturity* and *Golf Digest* magazines (just two of many) where retirement communities lure the readers with ads that read: "Florida living from $16,900 to $52,000 — your choice of three active adult retirement communities," or "Individual Retirement Homes — a continuing care retirement community of individual homes located in beautiful southern Ohio." When you see ads like these, call the toll-free numbers and ask for information.

Now, we come to a very interesting question: "What about moving out of the country?" Many retired couples do and love it. If you are considering this option,

I heartily recommend a book called *Travel and Retirement Edens Abroad* by Peter A. Dickinson. His book gives examples of countries with low costs of living, such as Hungary (the lowest), Mexico, Yugoslavia, Poland, the Philippines, Andorra, Dominican Republic, Czechoslovakia, Costa Rica and Canada. For example, $50,000 will buy a gorgeous home in Acapulco, or a two-bedroom condominium on a golf course in San Jose, Costa Rica.

In actuality, most retired American citizens who don't live in the U.S. live in Canada, Mexico, Italy, Germany, Greece, the Philippines, Portugal, Ireland, Israel and Spain. They're all worth your consideration.

There are all kinds of moneysaving reasons to move out of the country, many of which are tax-related. But you should realize that unless you give up your American citizenship you'll remain under the jurisdiction of the U.S. government and will be required to file a U.S. tax return.

If retiring abroad sounds appealing, check it out. It's definitely an idea for the couple completely free of trappings. If you have elderly parents who need you close by, or if your children still depend on you, this life-style is probably not for you.

The main thing to remember is that once you have selected a retirement life-style, there *is* a community out there somewhere that will give you that life-style on your income. After reading this book, you'll know what you can afford on the retirement budget you have available. You'll find that your money will stretch further than you thought, and the retirement life-style and locale of your dreams may well be within your grasp.

Chapter Two

A Place to Lay My Head

[Affordable Retirement Housing]

Now that you've chosen your retirement life-style and locale, we come to the next important decision: your housing. What kind of housing suits your new life-style and, most importantly, can you afford it? We need to find the perfect place to lay your head, but we need to keep your *total* housing costs, including utilities, taxes and insurance, to no more than 30 percent of your take-home pay. We'll cover tax and insurance problems in Chapter Six, but right now, use the following formula to calculate your monthly housing cost: Monthly take-home pay × .30 = monthly housing budget. For example, $1,400 × .30 = $420.

Your housing needs will take the biggest bite out of your budget, and to keep your total housing costs at this 30 percent level, you may decide to move to one of the low-cost states that are mentioned in Chapter One.

According to statistics, by retirement age most of you have your mortgage paid off on your present home, or are very

The average price of a retirement condo in McAllen, Texas, is $30,000.

close to it. Should you sell your home, take the equity, and purchase a retirement home that exactly suits your needs? This is one of the biggest questions faced by new retirees.

Remember that, depending on the life-style you've chosen, your home will be more or less important to you as a shelter. If you plan to be away from your home a great deal of the time, not only when traveling but during the day as well, it may not need to be as large or comfortable as it would if your home is also your recreation and entertainment center. If you're looking forward to working on your hobbies, or starting a small business out of your home, you need a comfortable place to spend your time. Your housing choice will be much more than a clinical decision. You should be able to live in a home that is affordable and practical, and yet makes you glad to be able to go home at the end of the day.

Seventy percent of retirees own their own homes. Many should sell, put the money to better use by purchasing housing that is smaller or more carefree, and invest the leftovers. However, there's a retirement disease among us called "Indecision," and most of us stay put rather than make the best use of our available assets. If you happen to be fifty-five, you may well live another thirty years, so there's no reason why you should get by in the old homestead if it's wrong for you. Let's look at your many options:

Retirement Communities, $30,000 and Up

You can purchase a mobile home, manufactured home, condominium or single family home in a retirement village that comes complete with a given life-style.

The costs vary considerably, but whether you love the desert, ocean or mountains, an affordable community is out there for you. Some couples like to golf, dance, play tennis, swim, fish, hike, water-ski, or do it all, and these activities are easily available on a budget. Even though the facilities may include a multimillion dollar clubhouse, two eighteen-hole golf courses, and more, the actual housing costs can run in the $30,000-plus range. Residents of these communities love them. They like the community life of sports, hobbies, crafts and activities, and they feel these communities are safer and friendlier than normal neighborhood living. As soon as they move into their community, they feel they have a part in the ongoing program of activities, and they develop an instant circle of new friends, which prevents the loneliness that can be a problem for retirees.

As I mentioned in the last chapter, I visited several of these retirement communities as I researched for this book. While I was in the Fort Myers area, I actually lived among the retirees at Pine Lakes Country Club in North Fort Myers. This is a well-planned retirement village complete with all the amenities you could hope for: an eighteen-hole golf course, tennis, biking, shuffleboard, swimming, fishing and gobs of planned activities, crafts and classes. It's clean and safe with homes starting at about $70,000.

I was equally impressed, however, with the community at Sun City Tucson, which boasts all the amenities found in Del Webb retirement towns. One of the days I was there, the men's golf group was having its annual club championship golf tournament. It was great fun to watch the men as they got ready to tee off. They were all jabbering at once, some about their hooks, others their slices, but all wanted to win—that was obvious! Meanwhile, a large group of women had assembled in the main building for their weekly hula lesson. Others were exercising in the gym while watching their favorite game show on television. Everyone seemed so into it all. It made me wish I was one of them so I could be having as much fun!

Here is a sampling of housing costs of a few retirement communities around the country:

• *Site-built homes starting at $26,000 in Lake City, Florida.*
• *A manufactured home for $21,900 in Ocala, Florida.*
• *A Spanish-style adobe home for $80,000 in Deming, New Mexico.*

• A one-bedroom, one-bath villa for $39,900 in a country club resort in Myrtle Beach, South Carolina.
• A detached home on the eighteenth fairway, near the ocean, for $88,900 in North Myrtle Beach.
• A 1,300-square-foot mobile home in a retirement community in Turlock, California, for $33,500.
• A two-bedroom condo for $45,900 at a golf resort in Chandler, Arizona.
• A custom-built home for $51,000 in Grand Junction, Colorado.

Retirement community housing runs in the $50,000 to $60,000 range in Washington and Oregon, too, as well as other low-cost areas of the U.S. If you've been living in one of the high-cost areas of the country, these prices will seem astoundingly low, especially when you see what you get for the money. If you're retiring on a small budget, making a move to a low-cost area may be necessary for you to make it. Let your children and grandchildren come visit you; it will be a nice vacation for them anyway. The alternative is to remain in your high-cost area and spend more than the recommended 30 percent for your total housing costs.

For specific names of retirement communities in various states, refer to a book called *A Field Guide to Retirement* by Alice and Fred Lee. You can also write the American Association of Retired Persons (AARP) for their booklet called *Consumer Housing Information Services for Seniors.* (You can find the address in Appendix A.) If you really fall in love with one particular retirement community, *be sure* to rent a unit on their premises or close by before buying, and talk to as many residents as possible. This is the only way to get a real feel for the advantages and disadvantages. Meanwhile, call the local Better Business Bureau to see if there have been any complaints. After all of this, you'll feel free to make your decision. However, don't *ever* let a salesman pressure you into signing anything or making a deposit until you're ready. And be sure you receive a deed and clear title; have an attorney or title company handle the formal closing.

Condo or Townhome, $30,000 and Up

Condos and townhomes offer much to retirees, especially those who plan to travel a great deal. They're usually more economical than a single-family home because the large-scale construction of a condo complex (shared roofs, walls and heating facilities) reduces each unit's cost. You'll be able to purchase the same number of interior square feet in a condo or townhome as in a single-family home for about 10 to 25 percent less cost. When purchasing a unit like this, you not only have full ownership of your individual space, but you also have the right to use all common areas.

Condominiums and townhomes are appealing to two age groups—the younger first-time buyers and the retired. Both groups like the value for the money, and the retirees especially appreciate the maintenance-free exterior, for even the landscaping is handled by the condominium association. In the case of a condominium, you own your unit plus a proportional interest in the common facilities, such as the grounds and recreational facilities. You pay a monthly fee for the upkeep, which should be considered in your housing budget.

Before purchasing a condominium or townhome, be sure to read and approve the bylaws. If you have any doubts, get the advice of an attorney. You should also consider these questions:

1. What about sound control? Can you hear through the walls?
2. Is the complex restricted to a certain age group? Are there a lot of young children occupying the only swimming pool?
3. Are pets allowed? If so, are they a problem in this complex?
4. Is the exterior of the complex well maintained? How about the grounds and landscaping?
5. Is there adequate parking?
6. Does the complex have a strong, capable association?
7. Is there a limit on the number of rental units allowed in the complex?

Apartment Rentals, $250/month and Up

Finding a reasonable, yet comfortable, rental apartment may be the wisest decision for you. According to *Retirement Places Rated*, certain parts of the country have quality rentals in the $250 to $350 a month range, and this will obviously free up your capital for income production. As with ownership of a condominium or townhome, all exterior maintenance is taken care of for you, but without a maintenance fee.

Here are some questions to ask before renting an apartment:

1. What about sound control? Is there a lot of exterior noise? Can you hear through the walls?
2. Is the apartment complex restricted to a certain age group? Perhaps you would be happier renting a unit in a complex restricted to a minimum of fifty years old, or older.
3. Is the complex safe? Is there enough light at night? Is security provided?

Here is a sampling of cities that offer quality one-bedroom apartments for reasonable rents:

• *Harrison, Arkansas*	*$280*
• *Paris, Texas*	*280*
• *Grand Lake, Oklahoma*	*300*
• *Deming, New Mexico*	*320*
• *Eagle River, Wisconsin*	*330*
• *Lakeland, Florida*	*340*
• *Thomasville, Georgia*	*340*
• *Austin, Texas*	*285*
• *Oklahoma City, Oklahoma*	*280*
• *Houston, Texas*	*288*
• *Colorado Springs, Colorado*	*290*
• *San Antonio, Texas*	*300*
• *Wichita, Kansas*	*305*
• *Tulsa, Oklahoma*	*305*
• *Pensacola, Florida*	*315*
• *Salt Lake City, Utah*	*325*
• *Denver, Colorado*	*333*

Some of the highest rents are found in San Luis Obispo, California; Cape Cod, Massachusetts; Reno; Santa Fe; New York City; Boston; San Jose, California; Washington, D.C.; San Francisco; Ventura, California; Los Angeles; Hartford, Connecticut; Chicago; and Honolulu and Maui, Hawaii, where rents range in the $1,000 to $1,300 range.

Mobile Home, $10,000 and Up

Mobile home living is one of the most popular choices of retirees, with more than 35 percent of all mobile homes in the U.S. owned by those sixty and older. Some mobile homes are located in parks; others are located on purchased or leased land, or even on a corner of their children's property. They come in all price ranges and with varying amenities.

One negative about mobile home ownership is that you don't have the financial advantages you would have with ownership of a condominium or single-family home. Your mobile home will depreciate approximately 10 percent the first year and between 5 and 6 percent each year thereafter.

There are a few states where mobile homes don't seem to depreciate; they are Alaska, Arizona, California, Florida, New Jersey, Oregon and Washington. As a matter of fact, mobile homes are considered *good investments* in these states. I live in California and in my hometown mobile homes have held their value for the past six years.

Here are some questions to ask yourself before you decide to purchase a mobile home:

1. Where can I park it? Can I afford the monthly fee for a mobile home park?
2. How well is the unit built? What is the reputation of the company that built it?
3. If you do decide upon a mobile home park, how secure is it? How well managed? What amenities?
4. Is there an age restriction for residents of the park?

New Jersey has 945 people per square mile; Arizona has 23.

Not all mobile home parks are reputable. In fact, before you make the decision to purchase a mobile home at all, have a place in mind to park it. Be sure the park is well managed with adequate water, sewer and electricity. Also, look into the availability of cable TV, if you want it. Some parks sell the lots and charge a monthly fee for the services and amenities. Others will rent the lot to you, but charge a higher monthly fee. Monthly fees range from $60 to $400. It's possible to find a park that offers security, swimming pool, clubhouse and other amenities for under $125 a month.

Don't count on being able to park your mobile home on any lot of your choice. There are strict local laws regarding the use of land, so be sure the lot you have chosen has land-use bylaws that allow for the length and the type of mobile home you own.

Overall, a mobile home can be a very wise choice for a retired couple on a small budget; on a per-square-foot basis, the highest quality mobile home will run half to one-quarter the price of a traditional home. Another cost advantage is that a mobile home is usually taxed as personal property as opposed to real property. This means that your taxes will be lower, too. Maintenance costs are low, also, adding another reason to consider a mobile home. True, this type of housing may not appreciate in the state where you want to live, but all the other savings can more than make up for this fact.

How can you get a mobile home in the $10,000 range? By purchasing a used one offered "by owner" through the classified ads. Usually it will already be in place in a park. Whether purchasing a used mobile home or a new one, watch for adequate insulation, sturdy fittings and appliances and enough storage space. If a mobile home has the seal of the Mobile Home Manufacturers Association or the Trailer Coach Association, you can be sure it has met minimum standards. There's also a booklet you should read titled *How to Buy a Manufactured (Mobile) Home*. It's another one of the consumer booklets available through the U.S. Consumer Information Center. Ask for booklet No. 423X, and send 50 cents to: R. Woods, Consumer Information Center-V, P.O. Box 100, Pueblo, CO 81002.

Single Family Home, $48,000 and Up

Perhaps it's wise for you to sell your big family home and purchase a smaller home for your retirement. There are many advantages to this idea. First of all, it will free up your surplus capital for investment income. It will appreciate, rather than depreciate, as is the case with most mobile homes. Everything about a smaller home will cost less, including the taxes, maintenance and utilities, but you'll still have a freestanding home of your own in the location of your choice. Again, you'll need to consider the states that have low overall housing costs to keep your purchase in the $40,000 price range, but it's worth it if you want to live within your retirement income.

As this book goes to print, you can purchase a nice retirement home in Peoria, Illinois, for $48,000; Oklahoma City for $50,600; Spokane, Washington, for $52,000; Mobile, Alabama, for $58,700; Louisville, Kentucky, for $59,300. The city with the highest median price is Honolulu, Hawaii, at $290,400.

Here are a few questions to ask when considering the purchase of a single family home:

1. How is the location? I'm sure you've heard that realtors always say the three most important factors in the value of a home are: "Location, Location and Location."
2. How is the crime in the neighborhood? Check with the local police department and ask the neighbors.
3. Are homes appreciating in the neighborhood? Ask a local realtor and talk to a few neighbors.
4. How well is the home built? Will it need expensive repairs in the near future?
5. Does the home have all city services, such as trash pickup and street maintenance?

As with any type of housing choice, if it means a move to another city or state, go there for a visit before making such an important decision. Better yet, try to rent for a while to get a real feel for the area. And, don't forget to budget the cost of moving, especially if you decide to move to another state.

Home Sharing, $20,000 and Up

Many retirees are unaware of the benefits of home sharing. There are many ways to do it. One is to charge rent to other retirees who will share access to your home. Another is to actually purchase a larger home on an equity-share basis with one or two other retired couples. Some homes are so arranged that they can easily be split down the middle, giving each couple privacy. Or, how about a duplex, triplex or fourplex?

You may think this is a novel idea, but it's actually an old one. Remember when America was a rural economy? It was common then for three generations to live under the same roof, sharing chores and expenses. How times have changed. We've become spoiled; we each want our own separate roof. However, if you're a retiree looking for a logical way to reduce your housing costs, what better idea than to share the costs with other retirees?

If two or more retired couples live in one large home, each can have a private bedroom and bath, sharing the kitchen and other common areas of the property. This will obviously cut your housing expenses by half or two-thirds. This idea can work for you whether you already own a home outright and charge rent to others, or whether you decide to pool your resources with others to purchase a home together.

There are fringe benefits with any of these arrangements, too, including a degree of security, shared maintenance time and expense, and the companionship of other retirees. Just think how carefree you would feel to leave on a vacation knowing your home was being watched over by your homemates. In any case, this is an alternative that should at least be considered since it is less expensive than single-home ownership.

In a recent poll that was conducted by AARP, 16 percent said they would consider the idea of home sharing. It might work for you.

In addition to the questions you should ask when purchasing a single-family home, here are some additional considerations:

1. *Can you live in the same home with another person or another couple indefinitely?*
2. *Are your life-styles compatible?*
3. *Can you count on the others to pitch in and help out with the interior and exterior maintenance of the home?*
4. *Do you have similar standards when it comes to housekeeping?*
5. *How about your transportation needs? Do all of you have independent means of travel so someone won't be stuck playing taxi?*
6. *How about pets? If the other couple has a darling little dog who loves to bury things in the pansy bed, that won't make you very happy if you enjoy gardening.*

Life Care Retirement Community, $20,000 and Up

If you're older when you retire, or in poor health, or just want to be sure health care is available now (when you are in good health), and later, if your health fails, you may want to consider the total life care concept. Many of these plans offer various types of housing, from independent living to total health care.

Bristol Village in Waverly, Ohio, is a typical life care community, where you can have the independence of living in your own home, but with the availability of continuing care. Their prices start at $20,000 and go up to $65,000. In addition to single homes, they offer Assisted Living apartments and a skilled nursing center. They have an indoor swimming pool, fitness center, and all kinds of fun programs for the residents.

One of the couples who bought in Bristol Village moved from Ann Arbor, Michigan. They feel the southern Ohio location has a much milder climate than Ann Arbor, and they love all the activities, including square dancing, craft and water exercise classes. Eight different couples who recently moved to Bristol Village were interviewed; they're all active and contented, but like the assurance of health care for life. And they've done it on small retirement budgets, too.

There are variations of this particular facility available all over the country, and some are obviously available only to the wealthy. However, if you really look around, you can find something affordable. One excellent source is your own religious denomination's life care facilities. Most denominations have a facility similar to Bristol Village, although it may mean moving to another state.

If you find a facility that appeals to you, just ask these three questions:

1. Will this type community seem confining after the first few years?
2. If so, is there a way to sell and change your housing life-style without losing your equity?
3. Is the community upbeat with happy residents?

Self-Contained Apartment on Children's Property, $25,000 and Up

Many couples offer to add a separate apartment to their children's home at a cost of $25,000 to $50,000. This is very cost-effective and will add to the eventual appreciated value of the home as well.

An apartment can be added over the garage, in a portion of the basement level, or a new wing built altogether. In any case, the obvious key here is how well the children and parents get along. If your family is the Walton's type, this just may be the answer for you.

Sale-Leaseback or Reverse Mortgage, No Outlay of Cash

These two innovative plans enable the retirees to stay in their own homes while actually liquidating needed assets from the equity in their homes. These plans are especially good for those who can't part with the old homestead.

A survey of 1,514 Americans, conducted for AARP by Market Facts, Inc. found that 86 percent of Americans fifty-five and older want to live in their present homes and never move. They hold a great attachment to the home where they raised their families, surrounded by their own furniture and keepsakes. For these retirees, the Leaseback or Reverse Mortgage may be the answer.

In the case of a Sale-Leaseback, you sell your home to an investor who agrees in writing to lease the home back to you for a designated number of years at an agreed-upon lease fee. If you can afford the monthly expense to lease the home back, you'll have full cash out of your home to use for living expenses or for other investments.

A Reverse Mortgage also gives you income while allowing you to stay in your home. This type mortgage is available to anyone sixty-two or older who owns his home outright. There are three types of Reverse Mortgages: *FHA-Insured*, *Lender-Insured* and *Uninsured*. A mortgage is created as you're being paid the monthly sum, and when the home is eventually sold, the equity will be less by the amount of the mortgage at that time. In other words, the longer you live in your home collecting this monthly income, the less your equity in the home.

Just to give you an idea of how the Leaseback and Reverse Mortgage work, here are a couple examples.

Let's look at a Sale-Leaseback on a home valued at $100,000. In this case you give up ownership by actually selling your home to someone who will become your landlord. In the initial sales contract on your home, the purchaser (your future landlord) agrees to purchase your home, pay you in full, and lease it back to you at a certain amount per month. By using the age-old real estate "Rule of 156," you can estimate your monthly lease payment by dividing the market value by 156. For example, if your market value is $100,000 and you divide it by 156, you will find that your monthly payment to the landlord will be approximately $641.

The advantages of the Sale-Leaseback idea are that you can stay in your home, you will "cash-out" your equity, and your landlord will pay for all repairs and upkeep. The disadvantages are that, unlike the Reverse Mortgage, you will *make* a monthly payment instead of *receive* one, and your new landlord will be the one who gains the appreciation on the home's value.

Now, let's examine an FHA-insured Reverse Mortgage at 10 percent interest on a home of the same value. After paying an origination fee of 1.5 percent and closing costs of about .5 percent, you can receive income from your equity in three different ways:

1. *Tenure: You could receive $352 per month income.*
2. *Term: You could receive from $372 up to $801 per month income.*
3. *Line of credit: With this form of payment you would receive a line of credit of $37,600, with no monthly income payments. You could receive it all at once or you could draw on it as you need it.*

The thing to remember with a Reverse Mortgage is that no repayment is required until you die or sell your home, and you *do* retain ownership of the home.

For a complete explanation of the Leaseback and Reverse Mortgage plans, order a forty-seven-page book published by AARP called *Home-Made Money*. See Appendix A for the AARP address.

Home-on-Wheels or Water, $8,000 and Up

Many couples are so thrilled to be out from under the stress of job, family and home upkeep, they make a really wild decision: sell the old homestead and live in a large recreational vehicle or houseboat. They know they can always settle down in a permanent abode again someday, whether it be a condo, mobile home or townhome in a retirement community; but, for now they want to feel free and unencumbered.

I can understand this need for uninhibited freedom; many of my days are filled with more than adequate stress to run me out of town!

Just think—no more house taxes, no home maintenance, no lawns or gardens to manicure, no city utilities, no salesmen at the door! What a life! Some couples take their motorhome or houseboat from place to place, as the spirit moves them, exploring and sightseeing as they go. Others settle in on a lake of their choice, or on the ocean or along a quiet mountain stream. Still others really do it right by parking on the Arizona desert in winter and alongside a Minnesota lake during the summer. Some retired couples even

belong to RV clubs that travel in caravans together, parking at prearranged sites along the way.

The retired couples I interviewed agreed that it takes a motorhome at least twenty-four feet long to be able to live in it year-round. Many retirees manage in eighteen footers, but the bigger the better if it's your only home. If you watch for repossessions or distress sales, you can find a dependable twenty-four footer for under $8,000.

One word of caution: If you decide you like this idea, be prepared for high yearly maintenance and repair bills, unless you can find a unit that is new or close to it.

Houseboat living has become more and more popular with the advent of aluminum and fiberglass hulls. The maintenance is low, and they are at least as comfortable as a nice mobile home. Many retirees love this kind of life, because a houseboat costs much less than most other kinds of housing, the upkeep is easy and inexpensive, and they can have a change of scenery on a whim, without ever leaving home. Don't forget that most houseboats can also be pulled by a vehicle to double as a home or camper on dry land.

Those who love the houseboating lifestyle seem to draw peace and serenity from living on a bay, river or lake. Water somehow provides a feeling of isolation from the stresses of life. Water communities of houseboats are tucked here and there all over the country.

Right in the center of Seattle, Washington, for example, 440 houseboats are hooked up to a legal moorage site, with all the city advantages, including telephone, electricity and special sewage.

There are lovely gardens along the shoreline, and the residents of these houseboats care and look out for each other. "Water people" are a special breed, and if you think you may be one of these, consider this alternative retirement housing choice.

Here are two recent houseboat ads:

Houseboat, 10' × 30', Kayot—holding tank & considerable renovation. 70 hp engine w/approx. 75/hrs. Excellent Delta berthing. $8,500/bo. Shown by appointment.

*

43' Houseboat, set up for live-aboard, twins/generator, radio, $15,000.

Here are some very important questions to ask before making the decision to live in an RV or houseboat:

1. Are you willing to give up a permanent home?
2. Will you miss your yard and garden?
3. Will you miss your neighborhood— neighbors, shopping and churches?
4. Will you miss having a garage?
5. Will you tire of the novelty of this carefree life-style?
6. Will you miss your things such as your antiques, or the grand piano, or your library?

Buy or Rent in a Foreign Country, $100/month and Up

As we already discovered in Chapter One, housing can be extremely reasonable in some foreign countries. This is definitely an option, especially for the retired couple who wants to stretch their small retirement budget as far as possible.

Guadalajara, Mexico, is a good example of economy retirement. One couple lives on $585 a month total for the two of them. It breaks down like this:

• *Total housing (including rent, utilities, telephone and maid)*	*$200*
• *Food, beverages and eating out*	*200*
• *Car expenses (total costs for two cars)*	*105*
• *Medical and dental expenses*	*5*
• *Barber and beauty shop*	*8*
• *Miscellaneous (newspapers, etc.)*	*40*
	$585

They say a couple can live *really* well in Guadalajara for $1,000 a month total.

Refer to the book *Travel and Retirement Edens Abroad* that I recommended in Chapter One, and you'll have all the details you need regarding retirement costs in various countries. It's a very honest book published by AARP, and it will not only give you the pros of foreign retirement, but the cons as well. It's *must* reading if you're considering living abroad as an alternative.

Here are a few serious considerations you should make before moving to a foreign country:

1. Will you miss seeing family and friends regularly?
2. How politically stable is the country

you're considering?
3. Is there quality health care available?
Do you have health problems that require medical specialists?
4. How safe are the foods and drinking water?
5. Is the crime rate high in the location you're considering? Will your home be safe? Will you be safe?
6. Can you adjust to any weather extremes?

The Big $125,000 Decision!

If you own your home now and decide to sell it to opt for any of the housing alternatives I've suggested in this chapter, you need to make the "$125,000 decision."

If you or your spouse have reached age fifty-five, and you have owned and used your home as your principal residence for at least three of the five years ending on the day you sell your property, you can elect to exclude up to $125,000 profit from capital gains tax. You can claim this exemption only once, so you must decide when to use it.

If you sell your present home and purchase a more expensive one, it's wise to delay taking this exemption until another sale, since your capital gains tax will be postponed anyway. So, you'll probably want to take advantage of this $125,000 exemption against the sale that will bring you the most profit.

In other words, you'll probably want to take this onetime tax exemption when you're selling the most expensive home you plan to own after age fifty-five. Usually, a couple takes this exemption when they're "moving down" from their $120,000 home to a $50,000 condominium, for example. This way they avoid paying capital gains tax on the profit from their $120,000 home.

In reality, because the median price of a home in the United States is approximately $92,800, you probably won't need to take the entire $125,000 exemption; however, those couples selling homes in the San Francisco-Oakland Bay area, for example, will find the $125,000 figure falls short of their needs, since their median price runs about $260,600.

Your housing decision will be the most important factor in your total retirement budget, so you need to give it plenty of time! Take it nice and slow, consider your options, and be sure of your choice. No longer are you forced to make instant decisions, like you did before you retired. Now you have the luxury of time—time to think about yourselves and what's best for you. Be a little selfish for a change—starting right here with your housing needs.

Remember—your best years are yet to come, and you deserve the very best housing you can afford.

Chapter Three

Wring 'Em Dry

[How to Lower Your Utility Costs]

Your 30 percent total outlay for housing should include your utilities, so obviously you must consider these costs, too, when deciding on

The average
...al snowfall in
...ny, New York,
...65.5 inches.
...enix, Arizona,
...s a "trace."

available right outside the front door. The national average for a cord of wood is $300; however, you can get it for free by cutting your own wood (get permission first) from fallen timber in local, state or federal forests. The typical yearly heating bill using wood is $350.

According to the U.S. Bureau of Labor Statistics, Consumer Expenditure Survey, the average total outlay for utilities for those fifty-five to sixty-four years of age is $1,901 per year. For those sixty-five to seventy-four years of age the average is $1,597, and for those seventy-five years and over it is $1,323.

As I interviewed retired couples all over the U.S., I found their average monthly utility outlay to be approximately $150. I thought there would be more variation from one end of the country to another, but the fact that Fort Myers, Florida requires more expense to run an air conditioner seems to be balanced by the fact that Oakland, California, for example, may have no expense for air-condition-

Belt, and western North Carolina, homes are heated with oil or kerosene with a typical yearly bill of $490.

Three million homes in our country heat with wood. Among retirement places, you'll find homes in Montana, Colorado, and Twain Harte, California, heated with wood because it's cheap and

ing, but higher heating bills.

The thing to watch for, I've decided, is the cost of that particular retirement community's or city's utilities. They can vary greatly within a state, so it is important to check out average utility costs in the city you're considering.

Lower Your Heating and Cooling Bills

Make sure there are no obstructions such as furniture or draperies blocking return-air grilles or heat registers.

If you have a gas-fired furnace with a standing pilot system, make sure the pilot is lighted, and the flame is steady and *burns blue.* The main burner should also have a steady, blue flame. If it's red or orange, you're not getting the correct fuel-to-air combustion ratio.

If you have forced-air equipment, change the filter. Filters are inexpensive and should be changed at least once a season.

Turn your heat way down at night and use an electric blanket. According to Northern Electric Company, it only costs seven cents a night to stay warm by using an electric blanket.

During the day, keep the furnace thermostat at sixty-eight degrees. Set the thermostat on your air conditioner no lower than seventy-eight degrees. Try wearing a sweater or cozy up in a snug sack in the winter; in the summer, strip down and use a small electric fan.

Shut off rooms you don't use very often, and block the incoming heating or air-conditioning vents.

Check seals on windows and doors.

Install new weather stripping or re-caulk if necessary.

Upgrade attic insulation. The Department of Energy says that this one thing alone can reduce your heating or cooling costs by 20 percent.

Consider investing in storm windows and doors. Heat loss can be reduced by half.

To save on heat, open the drapes on sunny days in the winter; close them at night.

In the summer, close your drapes during the day when you're using your air conditioner.

Use your fireplace as much as possible, or a wood-burning stove or insert, if you have one available. Try to cut and haul your own wood. (You need the exercise anyway, right?) Just be sure to keep your chimney flues clean. Purchase a stiff long-handled brush and cleaning kit from stores that specialize in fireplace and wood-burning equipment. This will prevent dangerous creosote buildup and soot accumulation that can interfere with the heating efficiency.

Lower Your Water Bills

When purchasing toilets or appliances, buy the water-saver type. Place a couple bricks in the tank of each toilet to save on water, too.

Landscape with succulents, rocks, wood chips and evergreen shrubbery. When you do water, do so for the minimum amount of time. Consider installing drip or mini-sprinkler irrigation.

Purchase a two and a half gallon

per minute low-flow shower head. ***Don't let the water run in the sink*** while you wash a dish or brush your teeth.

Lower Your Electricity Bills

Don't run your dishwasher or washing machine until it's full.

Check yearly energy costs when purchasing new home appliances. They vary considerably.

Wrap your water heater with an insulating blanket. You can purchase one at a hardware or home improvement store and easily wrap it around the water heater yourself.

Instead of baking in an all-electric oven, consider a homemade solar oven. More than five hundred people in Sacramento, California, have made their own solar ovens out of cardboard boxes, glass, foil, newspaper and glue. They can be used six to eight months a year in California. Most foods cook in about twice the amount of time that it takes in an electric oven as long as there are at least fifteen minutes of sunshine hourly. Temperatures inside the oven reach about 250 degrees, so food never burns or overcooks. Plans for building this solar oven can be ordered by sending $5 to Solar Box Cookers International, 1724 Eleventh Street, Sacramento,

The average monthly telephone bill in the United States is $45.33.

CA 95814.

Use lower wattage light bulbs and keep lights *off* except in the room you're using. Be careful that you don't leave porch lights on all night.

As soon as you move into your new retirement abode, call your local utility company. Some offer a free "Do-It-Yourself-Home-Energy-Survey"; others offer a complete energy analysis of your home for a reasonable fee, which will be recouped in the dollars you'll save in energy bills.

Some utility companies offer free insulation and other energy saving home improvements to seniors. These services are available to those customers who qualify based on their income. In California, Pacific Gas and Electric calls these services "Project Help." It's worth looking into to see if you may qualify.

If you're entering retirement with plenty of income, you may scoff at all my cost-cutting utility advice. But, the money you save (or don't spend) now means there'll be more down the line. However, if you have a small retirement budget to work with, but want the highest quality life possible within this budget, I'm afraid to say that you'll need to watch your utility costs carefully. If you've never had to be careful before, this will be a new challenge for you. But, after all, wouldn't you rather spend your money on fun stuff? Sure, you would, and you can!

Chapter Four

Don't Sweat the Small Stuff!

[Affordable Goods and Services]

That retirement budget seems smaller every time you review it. How you wish you had more money to spend, especially on those miscellaneous expenses that make life more pleasant. Well, I have wonderful news for you: you can cut your "goods and services budget" by 25 to 50 percent by using the ideas in this chapter.

First of all, what do I mean by goods and services? *Goods* are things like newspapers, gifts, books, magazines, stamps, stationery, cards, gift wrap, plants for your yard, cosmetics, Christmas presents, film, clothing, pens, calendars, notepads, fertilizer, etc.

Services are car and appliance repairs, dry-cleaning costs, gardening expenses, hair appointments, bank charges, seamstress charges, rug cleaning, watch repair, income tax help, etc.

You may have had no problem managing on your bigger pre-retirement budget, but now, with your reduced income, you need to learn for the first time how to stretch your spending dollars, especially

> *No need to spend precious money on copper cleaners; just use lemon juice and salt!*

on all this small stuff.

You see, the important thing to understand is that the *little things add up!* You'll be pleasantly surprised to see how cutting down here and there will give you the quality of life you want in retirement. However, I don't want you to live like a pauper, feeling deprived — no, not at all. But you will feel smart and smug as you "cheat the system" out of unnecessary dollars and cents. Trust me! You can do it. Here are the ways:

Buy On Sale

No longer can you walk into a store, grab an item, and walk up to the cashier to pay for it. If you're going to have a quality retirement on a small budget, you must look for sales — not the "pretend" sales where a price is jacked up 20 percent to be put "on sale for 20 percent off," but the *real* sales where you know the actual retail price of an item, and the sale price is not a "con."

Watch for these genuine sales advertised on television, radio, in newspapers, or by flyers at your door. And even then, shop with caution, watching for quality.

We have several major department stores in our area that have special sales about four times a year where customers get 50 percent off goods that have already been marked down a couple times. We watch for these sales because we can purchase clothing, for example, at 75 percent or more off the retail price. I purchased a dress outfit for my grandson recently at a sale like this. The outfit, which included slacks, dress shirt, suspenders and bow tie, had been retail priced at $39.99. The sale price that day was $18 with 50 percent more to be taken off "at the cash register." I purchased a quality suit for only $9. What a deal!

Another way to get items on sale is by using coupons. You've been so busy during your pre-retirement life that you may have thrown away those coupons that came in the mail, or at your door, or in newspapers and magazines; however, now that you have more time than money, start collecting them. I have in front of me this minute a coupon that arrived in a booklet in yesterday's mail. The coupon is for latex gloves, regularly 99 cents, for 29 cents a pair. Another is for Zee 150-count facial tissue, 59 cents for a box.

The whole idea of sale shopping can become great fun!

Buy Generic

Some consumer goods have generic equivalents; this is especially true in the drug industry, but it's also true in other industries as well. Most of these goods are sold under the store's label. For example,

Thrifty Drug Stores sells a 6.4-oz. tube of anti-cavity fluoride toothpaste for $1.59. The same name-brand tube sells for $2.32.

How about those appliances sold under the J.C. Penney, Sears or Montgomery Ward brands? They are manufactured by the same companies that produce the name-brand appliances. In a recent Consumer Guide "Best Buys and Discount Prices," you'll find that the Sears Kenmore brand built-in electric oven, for example, is rated tops as a "Best Buy."

Refer to consumer guides and read *Consumer Reports* magazine as well for comparisons of products. You'll find that often the best buy is a generic brand. By the way, go to your local library to do this research; don't spend your precious money on any books or magazines you can find for free.

Buy Factory-Direct

Factory-direct shopping has become a fad all over the country. Factory outlets are popping up on the outskirts of every major population area, as well as near the heart of retail shopping.

In San Francisco, for example, the Gunne Sax factory outlet store is located in a less-than-scenic part of town. You enter it from an alley, climb a couple flights of narrow stairs in an antiquated building, and finally open a door into a huge room of bubbling women pawing through racks and racks of clothes. If you want to try something on, you take it into a large open room where you strip down in front of the rest of the women who are squeezing and wriggling into their outfits. Women reveal personal attributes never before seen by human eyes for the sake of buying a $3,000 wedding dress for under $100. What buys you can get at Gunne Sax! True, there's no pianist to entertain you, and you can hardly walk between the racks of clothes, but look at the hundreds of dollars you can save!

Most factory outlet stores aren't this adventurous; in fact, they don't seem much different from most stores, but the savings are terrific. Items are regularly discounted 25 to 40 percent, but there are sales on top of that. You will be amazed!

Recently I shopped at an Oneida silver factory outlet store in Vacaville, California, where almost a hundred similar stores surround a huge parking lot. They had a sale on their flatware—10 cents a piece. The spoons were piled in one bin, the forks in another, etc. I had to sort through each bin to match up a pattern. There were five or six of us sifting through until we found enough of everything to make a set. I picked around until I found perfect pieces, unscratched, like new. Eight place settings at 40 cents each cost me $3.20! True, it took me quite a while to find pieces that matched and weren't scratched, but time is what retirees have plenty of, right? For the first time in your lives you have the luxury of the time it takes to find good buys like these.

There is a great new book on the market that will help you locate the outlet stores in your area; it's called *Fabulous Finds: The Sophisticated Shopper's Guide*

Clean your old cotton upholstery furniture with art gum squares purchased at any stationery store.

to *Factory Outlet Centers*, published by Writer's Digest Books. You'll save much more than the price of the book.

Buy Discount

Take advantage of all the discounts that are available to you. Starting at age fifty to fifty-five there are thousands of stores and restaurants that will give you a 10 percent discount.

If you join AARP, you'll receive 10 to 15 percent off many types of goods and services. It costs $5 to join AARP and is well worth it just for their magazine *Modern Maturity*. But the identification card you carry in your wallet will save you hundreds of dollars each year.

Carry every other kind of senior discount card you can, too. You may need to devote a separate part of your purse or wallet to these cards, but they're worth it.

Many department stores also issue cards for those fifty-five and older. They give the holder 10 percent off anything in the store one certain day each week even though the items may already be on sale.

Waldenbooks, the nationwide bookstore chain, issues a card to those sixty or older that entitles you to a 10 to 15 percent discount on purchases. Many other businesses offer the same thing, so *ask*!

Another way to buy at discount is to join a "Co-op" where you can buy all kinds of goods and services at wholesale.

Cable News Network recently devoted part of their Daywatch program to this idea. Call the National Cooperative Business Center at (202)638-6222 for the names of co-ops in your area.

In California we belong to Price Club and Costco discount buying clubs. We pay a yearly membership fee of about $30, which entitles us to purchase food, appliances, tires, clothes, office supplies, toys, plants, videotapes, etc. We buy our groceries at these stores on the first of each month, and while we're there, we watch for the *unbelievably* low prices on certain durable goods they carry off and on. We find a lot of our Christmas gifts this way, by shopping at some odd time of year. We hide all the toys and other gifts in our garage; then when everyone else is suffering from "pain in the wallet" at Christmastime, we gloat because our shopping is done.

Avoid the Malls

You knew I was coming to this, didn't you? You can't get factory-direct, wholesale, discounted, generic prices at a mall! Believe me, a mall is a dangerous place to spend your money and, unless you like to "mall-walk," should be avoided by the retiree on a small budget.

Before you retired, the mall made a lot of sense. You could go from store to store, using your credit cards for whatever you pleased. But no more of that stuff! You need to find *those same items* for sale at the factory outlets, co-ops, wholesale clubs, etc. I'm not saying you can't have quality, but you need to take the time you have to search for that quality in other places.

Garage Sales, Flea Markets, Thrift Shops

You've been so busy up to now that you may not have discovered how much fun these places can be. Look for garage sales on the "expensive side of town." I go to these sales all the time, and the wealthy do have better stuff to sell and sometimes ask less for it.

Last Saturday, for example, I went to a sale in the driveway of a very expensive home in our town, and I found high-quality hardback children's books for a nickel each. The original retail prices of these books were $7.99, $12.99, etc. I always look for quality toys and books to have around our home when the grandchildren come over. It would take an entire book in itself to name all the items you can purchase at garage sales. We have even found some fine antique furniture and jewelry. By the way, never be afraid to bargain. Start at half the asking price and go from there. The real "pros" do it this way: They gather up a huge arm load of things and ask if the seller will take a lesser amount for everything combined. Usually the person running the garage sale doesn't have the time or inclination to add it all up and just says "yes" because it sounds like a lot of money.

The same goes for flea markets, although the bargaining can become even fiercer. The idea of lumping several things together for one price works especially well at these places.

Thrift stores can be excellent sources, especially for clothing, but you need to shop around to find the real bargains. The L.M. Boyd column in our local newspaper recently reported that some of the best thrift stores in the nation are right near Beverly Hills, California. Evidently those secondhand shops close to the wealthy folks have higher quality goods.

Shop Through Catalogs

There are literally hundreds of thousands of catalogs out there. Some are "rip-offs," but most offer great discounts. Just be careful to comparison shop. Usually the sale catalogs for J.C. Penney, Sears and Montgomery Ward are very worthwhile. There's also catalog shopping directly through a warehouse, such as BEST Company, where you go into the store, find the sample merchandise, place your order through the catalog, then wait for your purchase to be retrieved from the warehouse. Remember that, although catalogs may offer discounted merchandise, it's even better to wait for the *sale* catalogs on the same goods.

There's catalog shopping for everything you can think of. One offers "factory direct grandfather clocks," and we're all familiar with the Heathkit Company catalog where you can purchase kits for building your own electronics. Or, how about the Craft King catalog that sells mail order craft supplies for 60 percent off retail? Another catalog I have in front of me shows a lamp for $29.99, the exact same lamp a mall department store sells for a hundred dollars more.

If you haven't paid much attention to the catalogs that have been inundating your mailbox, now is a good time to start. You need to stretch your money, remem-ber? Sure, it takes some effort, and it may not be as much fun as "dressing up to go shopping," but it will definitely get you the quality goods you need within your budget, and that's the whole idea.

Buy Used Through Classified Ads

Now, don't stick your nose up at this one! Have you ever tried it? If you ever do shop through a classified ad and find a real quality item dirt cheap, you'll be sold on this idea. The trick is to watch the ads every day, with several things in mind. Many items may be brand new, still in their original packaging.

Why are people dumping brand-new merchandise through a classified ad? Many sellers have gotten into a distress situation. A recent bride-to-be, for example, discovered that her groom wasn't all he was cracked up to be. Luckily, she found out in time, which meant that another bride picked up her size twelve wedding dress for only $200. It had been $1200 originally and was still in its zipper bag, tags hanging from the sleeves. The sales slip even came with it!

Buy Seasonally

Because of your hectic life before retirement, you probably never noticed that certain items are less expensive during certain times of the year. A new Reader's Digest Book, *The Consumer Adviser, An Action Guide to Your Rights*, reports that most retailers follow this yearly timetable:

•January: Coats, furs, diamonds, lingerie, cosmetics, luggage, televisions, radios and white sales.

• *February: Presidents' Day storewide sales, furniture, fur and hosiery.*
• *March: China, glass, silver, washing machines and dryers.*
• *April: Air conditioners, diamonds, sleepwear and lingerie.*
• *May: Memorial Day storewide sales, luggage, housewares, home furnishings and white sales.*
• *June: Father's Day promotion sales, sleepwear, lingerie and furniture.*
• *July: Independence Day sales, swimwear and gardening supplies.*
• *August: Garden furniture, furs, accessories and white sales.*
• *September: Labor Day Weekend storewide sales, back-to-school specials.*
• *October: Columbus Day coat sales.*
• *November: Election and Veteran's Day storewide sales, Thanksgiving weekend sales, coat, fur and furniture sales.*
• *December: Pre-Christmas sales and after-Christmas storewide clearances.*

Substitute Something Else

If you've always purchased things as you've needed them, this will be a really novel idea, but it *is* possible to "make something else do." Americans are so spoiled; they accumulate a surplus of material things, which is one reason, in fact, for so many garage sales. Their homes and garages are bulging with *stuff* and they want to buy *new stuff*, but don't have any more room. If you've been one of these spoiled Americans, now is a good time to learn some of the tricks used by our parents during the Depression.

Perhaps you're weary of hearing how your relatives had to sacrifice during that terrible time in history, but they had ingenious ideas, and it doesn't hurt to give them a try.

Make notepaper by cutting the backs off junk mail envelopes.

Save those tiny scraps of soap, soak them, liquify them in your blender, and use to fill your liquid-soap dispenser.

Save rubber bands, pieces of string, plastic containers, buttons off discarded clothes, etc. Just like Grandma used to do.

Make your own window cleaner by filling a spray bottle with water, three tablespoons of ammonia, and one tablespoon of vinegar.

Instead of buying drain cleaner, pour a cup of salt and a cup of baking soda into the drain followed by a kettle of boiling water. Works every time.

A personal note is warmer and more appreciated than the most elaborate card you can buy.

A newsy letter to a friend or relative may be more meaningful than an expensive long-distance telephone call.

Instead of buying a costly moisturizer for your face, just rub in a tiny amount of petroleum jelly while your face is still wet. Many expensive health spas use this treatment, but never reveal their secret. Even Doris Day does this!

Instead of expensive eye creams, place slices of fresh cold cucumbers on your eyelids. This will get rid of redness and puffiness.

Brush your teeth with baking soda.

Save the colored comic section from your Sunday newspaper to use as wrapping paper for children's gifts.

Wash your own car instead of paying to use a car wash.

Instead of joining a health club, use the free tennis and basketball courts at the park, and do aerobics with the fitness classes offered on television. Go for long walks!

Instead of buying windshield washer fluid, combine one quart rubbing alcohol, one cup water, and two tablespoons liquid detergent. This formula is guaranteed not to freeze down to thirty-five degrees below zero in the winter.

Instead of buying artificial silk flowers, revive your old ones by shaking them with a little salt in a paper sack.

Buy clothing that doesn't require dry-cleaning. However, for the inevitable wool coat or sweater, take them to a bulk dry cleaner where you can have them cleaned for $10 to $12 a pound.

Save money by avoiding debt of any kind, including credit cards. You'll not only save the interest charges, but you'll avoid impulse buying. If you can't pay cash for goods and services, you can't afford them.

Don't buy a new blouse just because your old one has a ballpoint pen mark that won't come out. Spray the ink with hair spray—it will disappear immediately!

Instead of buying bedding plants for your yard, start the plants from seeds inside your house. Fill plastic containers with dirt, plant your seeds, and water! You'll save gobs of money whether you plant flower or vegetable seeds.

I could go on indefinitely, but entire books give these kinds of ideas. One is *Mary Ellen's Best of Helpful Hints.*

My main purpose is to introduce you to the concept of saving money by substi-

tuting something else! This may be bizarre to some of you, but obviously you want to know or you wouldn't have purchased this book.

Learn How to Make It, Sew It, Fix It

Along the same idea as substitution, you should also learn how to do a few things for yourself. It's only understandable that you haven't had the time to do-it-yourself with the schedule you've been keeping all these years. You were lucky to find time to phone the plumber, much less learn how to become one. And I know you haven't had time to make a gift either. In fact, by the time you even thought of the idea, you were already two hours past your bedtime and lucky to remember to throw the laundry into the dryer before it molded. Ah, but now it's a different story because you do have the time, and time equals money.

Here are just a few moneysaving ideas.

Instead of running to the mall to purchase that anniversary gift, give instead a gift certificate good for a weekend of babysitting, giving the couple time for a second honeymoon.

Do your own gardening. Go to the library and read up on the subject. You might even like it! Use the flowers from your garden to make arrangements as gifts or a corsage for Mother's Day, etc.

Learn how to wallpaper, repair a leaky faucet, refinish furniture, replace an electrical wall switch, install a garbage disposal, replace a window screen, and clean your own rain gutters. If you've never tried to do these things before, check out a couple of books at the library or purchase a "how-to" video from Better Homes and Gardens (Box 11430, Des Moines, IA 50336-1430). Take a handyman class. Many are offered free over public service television, or sign up for an adult education class. The Consumer Information Center offers free and low-cost publications on many topics including home repair. Their address appears in Appendix A.

When it comes to repairing a washing machine, try a "fix-it hotline" before paying a professional to check it out. Average fees for washer repair are: Fort Lauderdale, Florida, $40; Denver, Colorado, $28; St. Louis, Missouri, $31; Manhattan, New York, $109. You can save these fees by fixing it yourself. Many appliance makers have toll-free fix-it hotlines for consumer assistance. They will walk you through the repairs over the phone. See Appendix A for a list of manufacturers and phone numbers.

Perhaps you used to sew or "craft" years ago before you became so involved with your career and family. Do you have any idea how much money you can save by making a dress yourself? Or a pair of slacks? Or your daughter's wedding dress? I recently priced the fabric and all the materials needed to make a certain elegant wedding dress. The total cost came to $106 for a wedding dress that would retail for over $1,000.

But how do you keep from botching it

up? Make the bodice of the dress in old sheeting first to be sure it fits and is becoming. *Then* go back to the fabric store and actually purchase the fabric and other materials, after you're sure the pattern will work and to give you confidence. This same theory works for anything you want to try, especially if you haven't sewn for a while. You can save 90 percent off the retail price of the same garment at the mall.

However, whether sewing, crafting or woodworking, if you can *enjoy* making something while saving money, what a wonderful use of your time!

If you've always gone to a hairdresser or manicurist, learn how to do your hair and nails yourself. It may mean an easier-to-care-for haircut, but you're ready for a change anyway, right? With your new carefree life, you might as well have a carefree hairdo. When I visited retirement communities all over the country, I saw some of the niftiest cuts on many of the women; the styles were not only carefree but youthful as well. It's the only way to go! And home hair coloring has become foolproof, too. Try it—you might love it.

Watch "Do It For Yourself" on The Discovery Channel and learn how to do your own electric work, plumbing, painting, carpentry and repairs.

Rent It

You don't always have to purchase an item just because you need it. If you need a "snake" to unplug a toilet, or, an extra tall ladder and scaffolding to paint the highest peak of your house, don't run to the hardware store to purchase one. Just rent it; you may never need it again.

If you get into the fix-it-yourself mode, you'll suddenly be needing a lot of tools that you never had. So, while you're waiting for them to pop up at garage sales, through classified ads, or at a flea market, just rent them. Don't become impatient and run out and purchase anything new. You're on a tight budget, remember? And besides, what's the use to save money by repairing something yourself, if the tools you need cost more than you're saving in the first place? Eventually, after a couple years of shopping for used tools, you'll build up a dandy workshop. What a good reason to hunt down garage sales — to find all the things you need to do-it-yourself.

Hire a Student or a Moonlighter

For those few times when you absolutely must have help, consider hiring a high school or college student or a tradesman who moonlights.

If you need help pruning a high tree, for example, rather than hiring a professional, just prune as high as you can and hire an athletic high school boy to climb that last ten feet. The same goes when you're painting the house, or repairing the roof, or lifting heavy bags of cement. Any time your body can't handle the physical labor, hire some help. Just be sure to look for the $5 an hour worker, rather than the $60 an hour professional. That student or moonlighter will appreciate the money, and you'll appreciate the savings on your body.

When it comes to car repair, take your auto to your local high school or junior college auto shop. It may take longer, but the work will be supervised, and you will save a gob of money.

Borrow It

Without becoming obnoxious, try to borrow saws, ladders, tools or whatever will help you get by until you find them for sale at reasonable prices.

Get the Goods or Services for Free

There are hundreds of goods and services available for free; you only need to be aware and on the lookout for these opportunities. Here's just a handful of suggestions.

I don't know how old you are, but do you remember the old-fashioned "barter system?" Believe it or not, it's still being used today, and retired folks like you need it more than anyone. It fits right into your life-style, because you have the time to make it work and the expertise in many services that can be bartered.

Here's how it works: Jack needs his income tax done; you need your computer fixed. Jack is a retired computer programmer, and you're a retired CPA, so guess what? You help him with his income tax, and he solves your computer problem. This is the informal, friend-to-friend method of bartering.

There are more formal methods of bartering, however, including barter clubs whereby members place "credits" in the bank. Each credit is equal to one hour's service. You may help several club members with their income tax, giving you a credit of fourteen hours of service, which you may then "draw out" as you need it in other forms of service from club members. You may need a valve job on your car or your kitchen wallpapered. See how it works? You can use your credits whenever you need goods or services available through your barter club.

Babysitting clubs have worked this way for years; ask any young mother. The mothers join a babysitting co-op where the hours they babysit other children become credits to be used when they need a babysitter.

To track down these barter clubs, see the General Resources section of Appendix A.

Always accept free samples of anything and everything. If you're in a store where they're giving away small vials of perfume, for example, accept them and ask for extras. The same goes for anything that's being offered for free.

Take advantage of coupon books that come in the mail. A book arrived in my mailbox today, in fact, that has two coupons offering items for free. One coupon is good for ten free plastic tube hangers with the purchase of $5 worth of groceries, and the other is good for a free photo album, if I bring a roll of film in for developing this week. I need the film developed anyway, and I can certainly purchase $5 worth of necessary groceries.

See how it works? You'll just have to get used to the idea of watching for "freebies."

Many services are free to seniors. One is the free tax help offered through AARP. See Appendix A for their address and telephone number to find out if this

is available in your area.

How about wood for your fireplace? It's available for free in many parts of the country if you cut and haul it yourself.

Get free pens, calendars, notepads, etc. by accepting promotional items given out as advertising. It doesn't matter that your calendar says "Hemingway Funeral Home" and your pen says "Remax Realty." You can even order free calendars through your U.S. congressman by calling (202)224-3121.

Rearrange Your Life So You Don't Need It

Does this sound like a depressing thought? It isn't really; it's just that you'll need to learn to rearrange your life so that it matches up with the goods you have available.

For example, don't take up snow skiing if it means purchasing ski clothes, skis, boots, a ski rack for your car, snow tires, chains, etc. It probably isn't worth it, even though you can find these things used through classified ads. There will still be expensive lift tickets, gasoline, parking and other costs. But, as an alternative, let's say you have access to your son's speedboat on a lake nearby with free docking privileges; why not take up water skiing? You'll need to buy used water skis, but the overall cost will be a fraction of snow skiing.

Perhaps the couple who wanted you to take up snow skiing with them is disappointed; make it up to them by inviting them over to play pinochle on Friday nights, or some other game you all enjoy. Or, they may decide that water skiing is a great idea for them too.

Rethink your priorities. If you have your heart set on the pursuit of something that costs money, try your best to come up with a substitute idea. Put your creativity to work!

Share the Cost With Another Couple

Here's one of the sanest suggestions in this book. Not only will it save you lots of money, but it will provide an instant friendship with other retired couples.

Many items can be purchased by two or more retirees. This idea works especially well if you're neighbors. How about these suggestions:

• Go together on a power lawn mower. Tom uses it on Saturdays, Jim uses it on Sundays. You use it on Wednesdays.
• The same goes for a rug shampooer. Several couples can go together on this item. In fact, the more couples, the better. If twelve go together, you can each clean your carpets a given month of the year.
• A video camera is another great idea. Several couples can go together on one camera, with an equitable arrangement for sharing.

Put on your thinking cap, and you'll come up with all kinds of ideas. You can share fishing equipment, a camper shell, camping supplies including the tent, dirt bikes, metal detector, and on and on. The important thing is that you purchase these things under a written agreement that not only spells out the shared use of the item, but the fact that *no matter who*

is using the item at the time of a breakdown all share in the item's repair.

This concept also works when renting tools or other equipment. We recently rented a video camera, for example. It cost $40 for a three-day weekend. We really only needed it one afternoon, so we could have cut that cost way down if others had wanted to share.

Do Without

Please don't go into shock! It *is* possible to do without something altogether, even something you think you really, really, really want. If you deny yourself once, it will be easier the next time, and you'll discover that doing without doesn't hurt nearly as bad as you think.

I know of one couple who decided to turn down an invitation to join three other couples on an Alaskan cruise. They really did want to go, but it would have meant borrowing the money, and they didn't want to do that. Their friends begged them right up until the last minute, and finally left without them; the couple went on a short camping trip instead, although they felt awfully blue about giving up the big trip. Well, as it turned out, their friends all got sick—they threw up the whole time. Meanwhile, they had a great time on their little camping trip despite their initial disappointment. You see, things aren't always what they're cracked up to be, and denying yourself once in a while is a smart thing to do.

And what about buying such expensive Christmas gifts? I know you're crazy about your grandchildren, but they'll appreciate that wooden puzzle you made by hand just as much as the Nintendo game they suggested. Children are spoiled nowadays anyway, and they need to learn they can't have everything they hint at for Christmas.

This is probably a good place to mention those cigarettes. Do you *really* need them? If you've been smoking a pack a day, you can save about $730 each year by giving it up, not to say anything of the money you'll save in health costs.

Beware of Frauds!

One of the easiest ways retirees can save money on goods and services is to beware of frauds — you know, the con artist who calls you on the telephone, knocks at your front door, or sends you enticing sweepstakes entries through the mail. You may think you're immune to this kind of thing, but, believe me, not only do statistics show that seniors are the most vulnerable to con artists, but my own surveys of retirees prove the same thing.

Here are some actual cons that have been pulled on seniors:

Letters from senior advocacy groups soliciting money; the envelopes and letters have official-looking symbols and language, misleading the senior to believe it's a U.S. government mailing.

Telephone pitches offering "get-rich-quick" investments, "ideal vacation certificates," or anyone trying to convince you that you've won a prize. Usually you must

Never give out your credit card number over the telephone.

purchase something to "win the prize," or you must immediately send money for the shipping and handling costs of the "prize." In one case, a Modesto, California woman was offered her choice of a forty-six-inch color television, a $5,000 gift certificate, or a $2,000 cashier's check. All she had to do was send $498.25 for processing. The money was to be wired in cash by Western Union directly to the name of the man making the phone call.

Solicitation by a "charity" requesting that your check be made out to an individual or paid in cash only.

Door-to-door salesmen who ask you to sign a petition, or free blood-pressure test forms, etc. By signing your name you may *actually* be subscribing to an insurance plan.

Mailings from "The Social Security Protection Bureau" (sounds official, doesn't it?) This is a fraudulent organization that promises you "valuable benefits" including a gold-embossed Social Security card, a copy of your Social Security earnings records, representation in Washington, D.C., etc. They want you to pay $7 for this service; however, the group has been singled out by the Senate Select Committee on Aging for fraud because the "copy of Social Security earnings" is nothing more than the government's own form to be filled out by you and mailed to the Social Security Administration requesting your record. The "representation" or "protection" afforded is unclear, according to Senator David Pryer, Chairman of the committee.

Beware of similar mailings from "American Seniors, Inc.," called a front for the Golden Rule Insurance Company by the House Ways and Means Health Subcommittee.

As incredible as it seems, people of all ages are still letting pushy salesmen into their homes. These salesmen are trying to sell asbestos spray, vacuum cleaners, aluminum siding, etc. In one case a man and woman knocked at the door. When the lady of the house opened the door, the man and woman stepped right into her home, and she couldn't get them to leave. Finally the man left, but the woman stayed. When the lady of the house insisted the woman leave, the woman said, "I can't, he's my driver." Three hours later the man returned, and the man and woman together tried an insulting "close." The man became angry when the lady of the house wouldn't buy the vacuum cleaner. He yelled at her, "Why are you hanging on to your money? Do you think you can take it with you?"

Another house-to-house trick is the "neighbor in trouble" routine. Someone knocks at your door, looks piteous, and asks for assistance. They call themselves "neighbors down the block." They say a relative has been injured, is in the emergency room of a nearby hospital, and could they have $35 to get the relative admitted? "Can you help out until the bank opens in the morning?" they ask anxiously. This usually works because the amount requested is relatively small, and few people want to turn down a neighbor in need.

Listen to this scam: You receive a post-card or letter informing you that you may have won a new car, cash or some other prize. They ask you to call a 900 number to find out if you're a winner. If you make this call, you automatically run up a charge—often $4 to $6—on your phone bill. In some cases you pay by the minute and are kept on the line. Usually you aren't one of the winners, but if you are, the prize is worth far less than the money they made off you on the 900 number phone call.

Another recent trick used by a thief is to pose as a Social Security employee to gain entry into a senior's home. Once inside, he gets access to checkbooks, steals checks, and persuades the victim to sign fake forms so the thief can copy or forge the senior's signature onto the pilfered checks.

I could go on and on, but you get the idea. Here is basic advice to prevent you from falling victim to the smoothies:

• *If it sounds too good to be true, it probably is.*

• *If you really have won a legitimate contest or sweepstake, you should never have to pay postage, make toll calls, or pay to receive your prize. If it's legitimate, everything will be free.*

• *Don't commit to donations over the phone.*

• *Never give out your credit card number to anyone, whether over the telephone, at the front door, or through the mail.*

• *Don't even answer the front door if it's a salesman or stranger. Just because someone knocks on your door doesn't mean you have to answer it.*

• *Have your telephone number unlisted in the telephone directory. There is a*

small monthly service charge, but the peace of mind is worth it.
• Throw away all the sweepstakes mail you receive. Don't even be tempted.
• Throw away all the mail from "charities" soliciting money.

This basic kind of advice is given every day, through AARP and other legitimate organizations, but seniors for some reason don't listen. Please do! You'll not only be spared the ordeal, but you'll be able to stay within your small retirement budget, which is my goal for you.

You need to ask yourself over and over again: "How can I accomplish this task without spending money?" This will be a foreign thought to you if you have always bought what you needed during your pre-retirement days. But you're in a different stage of your life now, and you need to save every dollar you can. It's really quite easy once you get the hang of it. Put a big fat rubber band around your wallet; when you reach into your wallet for money, let this rubber band be your reminder: "Don't spend any money unless you absolutely must!"

The retirees I interviewed for this book are already using many of the ideas in this chapter. Wives all over the country have learned to cut their husband's hair; gifts are made reasonably in crafts classes; couples are joining discount buying clubs; shoppers are using coupons; retirees are wary of con artists; and almost all of them love garage sales and flea markets. Many of them have taken classes to learn new skills that save them money, too.

If others are doing it, you can, too! Give it a try.

Chapter Five

Great Vittles!

[Tasty Nutrition on a Budget]

Here's something we all love to think about—food! What's for dinner? Isn't that the subject of the day? And when you're retired you have even more time to plan your meals. Retired Americans spend between 12 and 16 percent of their total budget on food, including eating out. To calculate your monthly food budget multiply your monthly income by .14. For example: $1,200 × .14 = $168.

Food is a very individual thing; many couples like to splurge on food and eating out and scrimp in other ways. Also, some couples like to entertain more than others. There was a huge variation in the eating habits and expenditures of the retired couples I interviewed. One retired man who lives alone spends no more than $50 a month on food. He purchases "legumes and beans" and cooks up four meals at once, eats one, saves one in the refrigerator, and freezes two. He believes in "no fancy breads," just the most inexpensive plain wheat bread with "no fancy oats or nuts or anything."

Citrus fruits, strawberries, peppers, broccoli, brussels sprouts and cabbage are good sources of the Vitamin C you need every day.

I interviewed one retired couple whose total food bill is $500 a month. They purchase $200 in food for home and spend $300 a month eating out. It's their choice to put their eating above travel or a newer car. Food could be considered recreational for this couple.

Statistics show that retirees have many of the same bad eating habits as the rest of the population. They go on "starvation diets"; or they buy anything they want regardless of fat or sugar content; or they cheat their bodies of nutrition by eating inexpensive foods that aren't good for them.

Is it possible for retirees to eat food that's yummy, nutritional *and* affordable? Yes, it is! But we need to know how to do it. Because this book suggests ways to stay on a tight budget, we need to find out what these economical foods are and how to prepare them for our best health.

There are seven major health organizations in the U.S. and they all agree on six things when it comes to healthy eating. The seven organizations are:

• *American Heart Association*
• *American Dietetic Association*
• *American Diabetes Association*
• *Centers for Disease Control*
• *National Heart, Lung and Blood Institute*
• *American Cancer Society*
• *U.S. Department of Agriculture and Health and Human Services*

Here are the six things they all recommend:

1. *Eat a nutritionally adequate diet consisting of a variety of foods.*
2. *Reduce fat consumption, especially saturated fat and cholesterol.*
3. *Increase consumption of complex carbohydrates and fiber.*
4. *Reduce intake of sodium.*
5. *Achieve and maintain a reasonable body weight.*
6. *Consume alcohol in moderation, if at all.*

What does all this mean? Even though we want to purchase foods we can afford, we must eat a well-balanced diet that consists of whole grains, fruits, vegetables, low-fat dairy products, lean meats and legumes. Try to stay away from sweets, alcohol, snack foods, gravy, salad dressings, fried foods, fatty meats, rich desserts and any other foods high in fat.

Your required fiber will come from the fruits, vegetables, legumes and whole grains, and your calcium needs will come from the low-fat dairy products.

One dietician I interviewed said that if people didn't eat fats, she would be out of a job. She said that we should beware of any foods that come from something that "breathes." Ice cream comes from cow's milk, and cows obviously breathe. Hamburger comes from beef cows, which also breathe. Whipping cream comes from, you guessed it—a cow! French fries are deep fried in lard which comes from—right again! When planning your menus and shopping lists, keep this simple idea in mind—did this ever breathe? Being aware of this one little concept can help your heart, arteries, teeth, bones, weight control, and even your resistance to disease, including cancer.

So, you've heard all this before—I know. You've made token efforts to eat healthier in the past, but were so busy with other things, you slid back into your old buying and eating habits, right? Isn't this a good time to make a few changes in your eating habits? Especially since you need to establish an affordable retirement food budget anyway, why not make this time of your life the best when it comes to your health? You'll live longer, too.

O.K. Let's say you agree with this plan and decide to buy more fish, skinless chicken, low-fat cottage cheese, fresh fruits and vegetables. How should you cook them? Here are the six recommended ways to cook your new healthy foods:

Microwave. This is a great low-fat cook-

Save money on your food budget by growing your own food. For information, write:
Senior Gardening and Nutrition Project
College of Human Development
University of Oregon
Eugene, Oregon 97403-1273

ing method. Use bouillon and wines for flavor and tenderness.

Broil, bake or barbecue. This also reduces fat by letting the accumulated fats drain away from the food.

Use your crockpot. Remember that round thing in the back of your cupboard? It used to seem like a great idea, right? Well, now is the time to get it out and look at your recipe book. Tough, inexpensive cuts of meat become tender, flavorful delights when cooked in a crockpot.

Steam. This adds no fat at all and conserves nutrients and flavor.

Pressure cook. This age-old method, like the crockpot, can convert tough cuts into delectable main dishes.

Poach. This leaves food moist and juicy and adds no extra fat.

I am of the firm opinion that a retired couple can eat delicious, nutritious, balanced meals for $45 a week, or no more than $192 per month. There are hundreds of nutritious weekly menus that will hold you to this limit, but here is one week's worth, just to prove it can be done:

Sunday

Breakfast — $1.25
  ½ small grapefruit each
  4 corn pancakes (prepared from mix)
  with ¼ cup pancake syrup
  4 slices crisp bacon
Lunch — $2.72
  2 cups New England clam chowder
  (canned condensed)
  Tuna on whole grain crackers
  8-oz. sliced pickled beets
  Cucumber and onion salad
  ½-cup cherry gelatin each

Dinner — $2.83
  2 shoulder lamb chops each
  Corn, green bean mixture
  Cold macaroni salad
  ½-cup chocolate pudding each

Monday

Breakfast — 96 cents
  ¾-cup canned grapefruit juice each
  ¾-cup cold cereal each
  ½-cup cold milk each
Lunch — $2.12
  American cheese and turkey bologna
  sandwiches
  made with 2 tbsp. diet salad dressing
  4 leaves of lettuce
  4 slices of whole grain bread
  2 bananas
Dinner — $3.21
  Cooked pasta tossed with broccoli and
  garbanzo beans
  with diet dressing
  Salad made of 2 cups lettuce
  with 2 tbsp. diet vinaigrette dressing
  1 pear each

Tuesday

Breakfast — $1.11
  ¾-cup orange juice each
  4 slices rye bread toast
  with 2 tbsp. honey
Lunch — $1.74
  Crockpot chicken-vegetable soup
  Chopped egg sandwiches with
  diet mayonnaise substitute
  and 4 chopped olives
  2 leaves lettuce
  4 slices enriched white bread
  4 gingersnaps
Dinner — $3.08
  Meat loaf

Mashed potatoes
½-pint cherry tomatoes, sliced and
gently microwaved
½ grapefruit each

Wednesday

Breakfast—88 cents
¾-cup canned pineapple juice each
4 slices whole grain toast
with 2 tbsp. strawberry jam
Lunch—$2.07
½-cup tomato juice each
Peanut butter and jelly sandwiches
on 4 slices dark rye bread
4-oz fresh strawberries each
Dinner—$3.14
Chicken thighs baked in mushroom
soup
Steamed snap peas
1 small baked potato each
½ apple each

Thursday

Breakfast—91 cents
¾-cup cranberry juice each
¾-cup cold cereal with
½-cup cold milk each
Lunch—$2.56
¾-cup apple juice
Chicken salad sandwiches with
chopped green pepper
diet mayonnaise
chopped onion
served in 2 whole grain pita shells
Fruited yogurt
4 gingersnaps
Dinner—$3.25
4-oz per person broiled flounder fillets
with lemon
1 ear of boiled corn each

with 2 tsp. margarine
Coleslaw
2 nectarines

Friday

Breakfast—$1.22
¾-cup orange juice each
1 English muffin each
with cholesterol-free margarine
and grape jelly
Lunch—$1.71
Tuna salad sandwiches made with
3 tbsp. diet mayonnaise
chopped onion
2 tsp. sweet pickle relish
4 leaves lettuce on
4 slices whole grain bread
Carrot and celery sticks
1 banana each
Dinner—$2.50
Chicken livers cooked in chicken bouillon in Crockpot
Steamed fresh green beans
with 4 tsp. diet margarine
¼ cantaloupe each

Saturday

Breakfast—85 cents
1 orange each, cut into wedges
1 egg each, scrambled
1 slice toast each
with 1 tsp. diet margarine each
and strawberry jam
Lunch—$2.20
Broiled breast of chicken fillet sandwiches
served with sliced tomatoes and
lettuce leaves
on French bread
with diet Russian dressing

2 cups lemonade
4 fig bars
Dinner — $3.56
   Buy 2 4-oz frozen cheese pizzas and
   top them with:
   sliced fresh mushrooms, cherry tomatoes, green peppers, green onions and
   2 tbsps. grated Parmesan cheese
   Serve with green salad made of:
   2 cups lettuce
   1 cup shredded cabbage
   ½-cup grated carrot
   with 2 tbsp. diet mustard vinaigrette
   dressing
   ½-cup vanilla ice milk each
   topped with ½-can crushed pineapple
   in its own juice
   4 gingersnaps

In addition to all this food, you can
have coffee or tea with or in between your
meals. The grand total for this week's
worth of nutritious eating for two retirees
is less than $45. Of course, there may be
a slight variation in this dollar amount in
your part of the country, but, if you're
growing any of your own fruits or vegetables, the total can be even less.

You'll notice how balanced this week's
menu is, with food from all four food
groups: meat, dairy, bread-cereal and
fruit-vegetable. Where seniors get into
trouble is when they eat only one or two
types of food all month because they
think it's economical. You can't eat beans,
rice and bread all the time, even if it will
cost you less than $50 a month. This is
your long-awaited retirement, and you
want to be healthy so you can enjoy it.
You'll see, too, when we get to Chapter
Eight, that taking care of your health will
mean fewer medical bills as well. So,

spend your food allotment on healthy
choices. You can do it and still stay within
your budget.

Be creative! Use nutritious, budget recipes and make up a rotation of meals that
you enjoy. Juggle it around, try out the
recipes, and then price them out until you
can eat healthily while still enjoying one
or two restaurant meals a week. An excellent source of budget recipes is a book
titled *Thrifty Meals for Two: Making
Food Dollars Count*. It has been prepared by the Human Nutrition Information Service. Write them for *Home and
Garden Bulletin Number 244*. This address appears in Appendix A.

Whether you agree with the nutritional
aspect of retirement eating or not, here
are ways to make your food dollars
stretch:

Pay Less for Your Groceries

Compare product information.
What are you paying per ounce or per
item? Look for the lowest price per unit,
not only within that particular grocery
store, but compare all the stores in your
area to see which one consistently has the
best prices. I did my own study for my
area of California, and I found that Albert-
son's ran about 9 percent more than
Lucky's; Lucky's 10 percent more than
Food for Less; and Food for Less 5 percent more than Costco (a discount wholesale food warehouse).

*Use generic substitutes whenever
possible.* For example, we feed a couple
of alley cats (just out of the goodness of
our hearts, of course) and we feed them

a generic cat food called: *Cat Food*. It comes in a big yellow bag with no writing at all except *Cat Food*. The cats really love it. The ten-pound sack costs about $3.50 compared to $11.50 for a name brand.

When you go grocery shopping, take a prepared list to prevent impulse buying. Also, never go to the grocery store when you're hungry or tired.

Buy foods that are in season or locally grown.

Purchase foods at local farmer's markets or right off the farm, if possible.

Buy in bulk as much as you can. You've seen the bins of pinto beans and black-eyed peas and flour. Just scoop out what you want, weigh and label it and save up to 75 percent off the beautifully packaged name brands.

Join a food club or wholesale food outlet, and when purchasing food in these places, buy in the largest quantities you have room to store. When we shop at Costco, we buy Breck shampoo, for example, in a giant gallon-sized container. We use it to fill our smaller shampoo bottles. We do the same with dishwashing liquid, and we purchase laundry detergent in forty-four-pound buckets. The detergent costs about $9 and lasts me two months.

Stay away from the prime rib roasts, t-bone steaks and racks of lamb. Satisfy your protein needs with less expensive selections: peas, lentils, beans, eggs, chicken.

Shop your grocery stores on sale days and purchase the sale items; don't be distracted by the bags of pretzels, gourmet imported cheeses, and other expensive snack foods on your way to the bread that's on sale.

Use coupons as much as possible and take the time and trouble to send in for rebates, too. I know when you were working, you may have only used coupons on a hit-or-miss basis, but you're retired now and you have the time to do it right. Purchase a check-sized expanding file with labeled pockets. Then you'll need to cut out all the little coupons from the magazines and newspapers. What fun you're going to have! Just think, you'll save hundreds of dollars this next year just because you use your coupons. Be sure to keep the coupons in your purse or as handy as possible so you'll be inclined to use them. They say that for every hour you spend clipping and filing coupons, you'll save $30 on your food bills. Just say over and over again: "Saving coupons is fun . . . saving coupons is fun . . ."

Look for simple packaging of food products; you'll pay extra for fancy, glamorous or gimmicky packaging.

Grow your own. Plant as many fruit trees and vegetables as possible. Plant more than you can use, and can or freeze the excess for the winter months. A really popular idea lately has been to grow your own herbs. You can do that right in your kitchen window year-round.

> *Granola bars are high in sugar, derive about one-third of their calories from fat, and aren't any healthier than a candy bar.*

Eat Out on a Budget

The first thing to realize is that fast food restaurants aren't the bargain they're cracked up to be. Let's take a typical meal at McDonald's for example. You go in and order a Big Mac, fries and a shake. The total price for these items will vary from town to town, but if you live in New York City you'll pay approximately $4.97. For that same price I can make four Big Macs, fries and shakes at home, or you can eat at a Kings Table Buffet for about $5, if you use their discount coupon.

One nutritionist discovered another interesting fact about fast food restaurants: they aren't nearly as "fast" as you might think either. She says that by the time the family drives to the restaurant, stands in line, orders, eats and returns home, they could easily have eaten something from their own kitchen. This particular nutritionist is very concerned, too, about the extra calories, fat and sodium contained in many fast foods.

Questions about food safety? Call the U.S. Department of Agriculture Hotline: (800)535-4555.

Use discount coupons whenever you can; they come in the mail and are in magazines and newspapers. For example, a coupon that is offered frequently in my area is good for two meals for the price of one.

Have your special meal out at lunchtime instead of dinner. A lunch will cost half or a third as much as the same selection on the more expensive dinner menu. Also, there are "Early Bird Specials," which means that you can have lovely evening meals for about half the regular price if you come "early" between 5:00 and 6:00 P.M. or whatever is required.

Bypass the alcoholic beverages when you eat out. If you really want a glass of wine with dinner, just grit your teeth until you're back home where you can share a bottle of Beringer White Zinfandel for the price of a single glass at a restaurant. Two bottles of this particular brand of wine sell for $6.95 at our local Costco. Besides, it's always safer to avoid alcohol until you're at home.

Frequent restaurants where it isn't awkward to split a meal. One Mexican restaurant we like here in California serves the biggest Fajita dinners you've ever seen for $6.95. We ask for two extra tortillas, and then we share the meat and other ingredients. We're so filled up from all the food we have to waddle to the car, and we're only out $3.50 a piece for a great meal in a restaurant that has at least ten times the atmosphere of any fast food restaurant.

Always, always make use of your senior citizen discount at the restaurants you frequent. Even if the discount is for those over fifty or fifty-five, and you feel funny asking for the discount card, do it anyway! It's like having someone else pay the tip to the server, because you'll usually receive a 10 to 15 percent discount on your card. My husband just turned fifty-five, and we're having a grand time applying for discount cards all over town, not only at restaurants, but at all the businesses that issue them.

Befriend All Gift Horses

Never be so proud as to turn down free food. There's plenty of it out there for the senior citizen and others as well. There are cheese, egg, and surplus fruit and vegetable giveaways, all easily obtainable. Usually these surplus foods are given out at the places retirees are frequenting anyway—city senior centers, churches or directly from the source. Watch for word of these freebies in your local newspapers and on the bulletin boards of your town's senior center.

Another gift horse can be a fund-raising dinner or luncheon. I know you've been asked dozens of times to purchase tickets to a boy scout enchilada dinner, or high school band hot dog lunch, or whatever. Although you may have bought tickets in the past just to be supportive, you never used them because you were too busy to even think about driving across town on a Saturday. Now, you're retired. You have plenty of time, so why not get that good enchilada dinner for only $2.50 a piece? You might even have a good time and meet some interesting people.

How about the SOSP? The Senior Opportunity Service Program is a federally funded program for seniors where they can get together for a well-balanced, hot meal five times a week for about $1.50 a meal. We have sixteen of these meal sites in the county where I live. My in-laws love these meals because they fit into their budget and are delicious. You can find your closest SOSP meal site by calling the Senior Opportunity Service office, listed in the yellow pages of your telephone book under "Senior Citizen's Services and Organizations." The SOSP also offers a publication for seniors called "The Senior Log." It comes out every other month, costs $10 a year, and lists all the meal sites in your area, in addition to other helpful nutritional information.

Here is the menu for a recent five-day period in my area:

A cup of most of the common varieties of beans has about 225 to 250 calories.

Monday

Cabbage roll, buttered potato, winter mixed vegetables, carrot-vegetable salad, French bread, pear slices, milk, coffee and tea.

Tuesday

Sausage patties, cream gravy, lima beans, Swiss chard, raspberry applesauce molded salad, biscuit, pumpkin bar, milk, coffee and tea.

Wednesday

Golden baked chicken with sauce, escalloped potatoes, carrot coins, spinach salad with beet dressing, rye bread, apple, milk, coffee and tea.

Thursday

Juice, chili beans, Scandinavian vegetables, cottage cheese and fruit salad, corn bread, butterscotch pudding, milk, coffee and tea.

Friday

Hot turkey sandwich, sweet potato, apple casserole, Brussels sprouts, whole cranberry sauce, whole wheat bread, banana, milk, coffee and tea.

Can you believe these meals for $1.50 each? And my in-laws have fun at these luncheons. There's singing and instrumental music. For the price, why not take advantage of at least a few of these each week?

Save Money by Making Your Food Last

If you purchase food in huge quantities, such as a twenty-pound hunk of hamburger, you need to divide it up and double-wrap it well before putting it in the freezer. Whether you're freezing meat, bread, fruit or vegetables, take advantage of sale prices on these items by purchasing ahead and freezing. Keep whatever freezer capacity you have as full

Keep your freezer at zero degrees or below and your refrigerator at thirty-eight degrees to prevent food from going bad.

as possible by bargain shopping.

Bags of dried peas and beans can be stored indefinitely in a cool, dark place. These are an inexpensive source of protein, so buy in bulk on sale when you can.

Don't let food go bad in your refrigerator. You had great excuses when you were working two jobs, singing in the church choir, and had three teenagers at home who crammed unidentifiable things into the refrigerator. It's no wonder the back shelves began to look like a horror movie. Ah, but no such excuses now. You have time to keep your refrigerator clean by eating all those leftovers before they go bad. It'll pay off in money saved each month.

Revive foods that seem to have "passed on." If you do a little study on the subject, you'll find that many seemingly stale foods can be brought back to life. Take brown sugar, for example. When it's hard enough to use as a weapon, just place in into your microwave in a covered container, along with a piece of bread or wedge of apple. Microwave on high for thirty seconds and you'll have soft brown sugar again.

If you have crackers or potato chips that have gone stale, microwave them on high for sixty seconds—they'll become crisp again.

To get juice out of a lemon that has been around too long, microwave it for fifteen seconds before squeezing.

When we get to Chapter Thirteen you'll see exactly how much various retirees are spending for food and eating out. Some of those I interviewed are spending so little on their total food expense, you may wonder how they do it. They seem to manage by having gardens and fruit trees, and they aren't shy about accepting food donations.

Other retirees seem to be spending too much on food, even to the point of sacri-ficing in other ways. How you do in this category will depend on how insistent you are on expensive cuts of meat and high-class restaurants.

It's all up to you — you can definitely eat healthily on $200 a month per couple if you really want to do it.

In any case, bon appétit!

Chapter Six

You Gotta Have Wheels

[Economical Transportation]

Wouldn't it be great if retirement meant your transportation worries were a thing of the past? No such luck! Your car will still depreciate each year, it'll still need to be repaired; it'll still drink gasoline, oil and other expensive fluids. The experts say that retirees should try to keep total transportation costs to no more than 10 percent of their monthly take home pay. To figure your monthly transportation budget, multiply your take-home pay by .10. For example: $1,600 \times .10 = $160. Retirees on a small budget need to cut these costs down as far as comfortable for them, and here are ways to do it:

For a fee, the AAA Auto Pricing Service will give you the real worth of a new or used automobile. (800)933-7700

Get By With One Car

If you've been a typical American family, you've always had more than one car. It's true that one may have been your "road car" and one your "putts-around-town car," but you've probably had at least two of these expensive toys at a time. Obviously, now's the time to get by with only one car, and if you plan to use your automobile for travel, you'll need one that's as roadworthy as possible. If you don't plan to use your car on the road, you may get by with one that's older and less expensive, just for running around town.

Purchase a New Car Wisely, If At All

Perhaps you've decided to buy a new car as you enter retirement, one that will be dependable for your traveling, economical to maintain and, of course, affordable. Is there such a thing? According to the new *Consumer Guide Best Buys of 1991*, there are good buys available in every category. They take into consideration many costs other

Before you buy a used car, call the U.S. Department of Transportation Auto Safety Hotline to see if a car model has ever been recalled. (800)424-9393

than the purchase price: cost of maintenance, warranties, reputation for reliability, and durability and safety record.

Here are their Best Buy recommendations in some of the categories:

• *Subcompacts: Honda Civic — $7,000 to $13,140*
• *Compacts: Dodge Spirit and Plymouth Acclaim — $13,000 to $15,500*
• *Midsized: Ford Taurus and Mercury Sable — $14,000 to more than $20,000*
• *Full-Sized: Buick LeSabre, Oldsmobile 88 and Pontiac Bonneville — $18,000 to more than $20,000*
• *Sports Coupes: Acura Integra — $12,000 to $18,000*
• *Compact Vans: Dodge Caravan and Plymouth Voyager — hovers around $20,000.*
• *Four-wheel-drive Vehicles: Ford Explorer and Jeep Cherokee — $20,000.*

The *Consumer Guide* that suggests these "Best Buys" also lists "Recommended" buys in each category as well. But there are many other books, magazines and publications that will also give you comparison information when you're looking for a new car. One of the best and least biased is called *New Car Buying Guide* available from the Consumer Information Center-V. This guide is printed by the U.S. government to help you when buying a new car, and costs only 50 cents. While you're at it, you may want to order *Gas Mileage Guide* for the current year, which is a free publication. The address appears in Appendix A.

In any case, take plenty of time before making this big decision, and look into the possibility of purchasing a "demo" or "fleet car" from your dealer. You'll receive a new car with all the new car warranties, but with a few miles on the odometer. Other sources of discount prices are through your union or credit union. Look into these possibilities; you may save thousands of dollars.

If you have the funds to purchase a brand-new car as you enter retirement, you should be aware that a new car will cost you more than the initial price tag. These are just a few of the ways it can cost more than buying a used car or keeping one of the cars you already own:

---

1. *Higher auto insurance.*
2. *Depreciation at the rate of 30 percent the first year.*
3. *Higher automobile license and registration fees.*
4. *Cost of extended warranty coverage.*

Also, if you don't have the cash to purchase the car, you'll have installment payments, which will cut into your limited monthly income.

Another thing to think about is that you'll lose the interest on any cash you use to purchase a car, whether new or not. Say you purchased a car even one year old, you would save the first year's depreciation of 30 percent. If you were to purchase a new $18,000 car at one year old instead, you would still have $5,400 left over to invest somewhere. That would mean an income of 10 percent a year, or $45 a month.

Find a Great Used Car

Most of the retirees I interviewed reduced their car population to one car, which is good, and that one car, in most cases, was the better of the cars they already owned. But for those retirees who decide to ditch all the junkers hanging around their garages and purchase the best used car they can find, here is some good advice:

Research* Consumer Report *magazines and other consumer guides for the best buys. These are available in your local library.

***Order* Buying a Used Car,** a publication from Consumer Information Center-V. The cost is 50 cents. It will give you good advice whether purchasing a used car from a dealer or an individual.

Have the car checked out thoroughly before purchasing. This can be done through most mechanics, automobile service centers (such as Sears), or through services offered by places like the American Automobile Association (AAA). If you happen to be a member, they offer a reasonable service that diagnoses everything about a car before you purchase it.

Compare the price being asked for a used car with the actual value as listed in a "blue book," such as the *Kelley Blue Book Auto Market Report*, the one used most commonly in California. Another one used nationally is called the *Official Used Car Guide*, which is published by the National Automobile Dealers Association. The easiest way to get information from one of these sources is to call your local bank or credit union. They know how to use these books and will give you the wholesale and retail values. This book adjusts for low or high mileage and all the extras a car may or may not have. My husband and I believe in buying good, clean used cars and our rule of thumb is to try to get it at the "wholesale" blue book price, which means that we usually must purchase "by owner." We have a car checked thoroughly before we buy it and have made good decisions because of it.

Many studies show that overall you're better off financially buying a good used car than a new one. Runzheimer International, a management consulting firm, did a comparison study between the costs of a new car versus a used car. They found that if you drive a new car 15,000 miles a year for four years, your projected cost would be 23.4 cents per mile, but the cost of keeping your old car over the same number of years would only be 12.7 cents per mile. Over the four-year period, you would save roughly $6,400 by keeping your old car.

Look for and read the "Buyer's Guide," which must be displayed in the window of all used cars sold by dealers. This guide will explain who must pay for repairs after purchase. It will tell you if there is a warranty on the car, what the warranty covers, and whether a service contract is available. Try to find a used car, whether purchased through a dealer or by owner, that has remaining warranty that can be placed in your name.

Check the reliability of the dealer

> *One of the least expensive new cars on the market in 1991 was the Hyundai Excel with a base price of about $6,200.*
>
>

with your state or local consumer protection agency or the state attorney general. Also, check the local Better Business Bureau to see if there are a large number of complaints against the dealer.

Ask your insurance company for a free guide to buying a used car. If you happen to be a member of AAA, they have one available called *Member's Used Car Guide*.

Cut Maintenance and Repair Costs

Now that you're retired, you finally have time to "baby" your car. Remember how frustrating it was before? You were always rushing off to work or to an evening meeting, and didn't get your poor car in for a lube and oil change the way you should.

Ah, but now it's a different story! Now you have time to do all those smart things to make your car, whether new or used, last a long time with as little out-of-pocket expense as possible. You've heard a lot of these ideas before, but now that you're retired and on a small budget, you must try them out:

Make your tires last by checking for underinflation, out-of-balance wheels and bad driving habits. By bad driving habits, the experts mean speeding, making fast turns, driving over curbs, hitting chuckholes, or riding on the edge of the road. Also, you'll want to rotate your tires every 6,000 to 8,000 miles; this will mean more even tread wear, particularly if you have a front-wheel-drive car.

Make your transmission last longer by changing the transmission fluid and filter at least once a year. The experts say this should make your transmission last 100,000 to 200,000 miles.

Make your water pump last by not over-tightening the belt.

Make your engine last by changing the oil every 2,500 to 3,000 miles. Learn how to do this yourself and purchase the oil at discount prices.

Save on gasoline costs in these ways:

1. *Drive a fuel-efficient car. These are the top ten gas saving cars:*

Vehicle	MPG City/Hwy
Geo Metro XFI	53/58
Honda Civic CRX HF	49/52
Geo Metro	45/50
Suzuki Swift (1.01)	45/50
Daihatsu Charade	38/42
VW Jetta Diesel	37/43
VW Jetta Diesel Turbo	37/40
Geo Metro LSi	36/40
Ford Festiva	35/42

2. *Carpool.*
3. *Combine errands to use your car less.*
4. *Slow down. Driving 60 mph uses 15 percent more fuel than driving 50 mph.*
5. *Avoid abrupt starts and stops.*
6. *Avoid excessive idling when warming up your car. Even in the coldest weather, thirty seconds of idling will do it. Just drive more slowly at first.*

For a free AAA booklet that suggests ways to save fuel, send a self-addressed stamped envelope to:
AAA Gas Watcher's Guide
Mail Stop 150
1000 AAA Drive
Heathrow, FL 32746-5063

7. Check tire pressure. Underinflated tires will lower gas mileage.
8. Check your spark plugs regularly. Misfiring reduces miles per gallon.
9. Keep your engine tuned up.
10. Purchase a light-colored car with light upholstery and tinted windows; it will use less gas because you'll need to use your air-conditioning less.

Take a class in car repair. They offer these classes through adult education schools, junior colleges or vocational schools in your area. Learn how to do everything possible yourself.

Collect instruction books on the repair and maintenance of your car. When someone asks you what you want for your birthday or Christmas, name a certain tool or tool kit you need to accomplish this do-it-yourself magic.

Select auto repair shops very carefully. When you do need the services of a professional, check for ones offering these policies:

---

1. Guarantee their repairs for ninety days or 4,000 miles, whichever comes first.
2. Return replaced parts to you, except those which must be returned to the manufacturer due to a warranty agreement.
3. Give a written estimate of the total charges before repairs are made; if the total will exceed the estimate, they agree to contact you for permission before making the repair.

You can check a shop's reputation by asking for references, calling the Better Business Bureau for a history of complaints, and watching for members of the Approved Auto Repair program as designated by AAA. The shop will have a sign posted showing it to be "AAA Approved Auto Repair Service." You may also want to read a book titled *Auto Repair Shams and Scams* by Chris Harold Stevenson, with a foreword by consumer advocate Ralph Nader. Nader says that motorists pay about $40 billion a year on unnecessary repairs, based on figures from a U.S. Department of Transportation study.

We want your retirement dollars to stretch, so don't be one who gets taken by a fraudulent repair shop.

Take advantage of free car inspections. Occasionally, free inspections are offered by car repair businesses. They are also available through AAA as a public service. They have bright yellow vans that motorists can spot in shopping centers or other locations. An auto technician will check your car's fluid levels, tire pressure, lights and other safety-related items, and use a tail pipe sniffer to make a fuel economy test. The test takes about six minutes. Repairs aren't performed but you're given a written record of the check results to take to your mechanic. The van has a big banner that says "Free Car Check." Call your local AAA office to find out when this free service will be available near your hometown. If one of these vans isn't coming to your area soon, AAA offers free car

---

According to the Credit Union National Association of Madison, Wisconsin, over a four-year period you can save $2,400 by buying a $12,000 car rather than leasing it.

counseling by phone. If you have questions about your car's mechanical problems, call toll-free, (800)652-1158.

Alternate Transportation

Ride the bus. Now, don't laugh; just because you haven't ridden a bus "since the war" doesn't mean it isn't a good idea. Try it before you decide. Almost all the retirees I interviewed use buses of all types—local, shuttle and city-to-city buses in their areas. This can save you so much money and how convenient— you don't need to look for a parking place. Ask for the senior discount card, if you're old enough. Let the bus driver dodge the nuts on the road while you read or knit.

Call Dial-a-Ride. Most cities and towns in the country have this type of mini-bus that will give you a ride anywhere you want to go for about 75 cents each way. It may be called something other than "Dial-a-Ride" where you live, but you usually must call in advance for an appointment for them to pick you up.

How about a motorcycle or bicycle? Get your helmet and away you go! If you haven't driven one of these two-wheeled toys in a while, be sure to practice. Talk about economy—and the bicycle will do your heart good, too.

Talking about your heart, how about walking! Now that's a novel idea, you say. You may be used to going for a walk, but it never occurs to you to *actually walk somewhere*. So the dentist's office is a mile away, the walk will be perfect for your health, not to mention that your mind will be nice and relaxed when you get there. The dentist will love that, too!

How about sharing rides with others going to the same meeting or event? One week you drive; one week the other person. It adds up at the end of the month. Remember— every time you leave your car in the garage, you leave dollars in your wallet!

Most of the retirees I interviewed are very careful to keep their transportation costs low. As a matter of fact, they seem to be much more interested in cutting down on transportation costs than on food budgets. Residents of the retirement communities I visited were determined to walk, ride bicycles, and "take the bus to town." All these choices left their clean, shiny cars parked safely and economically in their carports and garages. They all seemed determined to make their cars last.

You will see exactly what some of these retirees spend when we get to their budgets in Chapter Thirteen.

The conclusion seems to be that you can keep your transportation costs under the recommended 10 percent of your income. All you need are your sun hat, walking shoes, and a couple of bicycles. Other retirees are doing it, and so can you.

The average cost of a minor tune-up is $60 to $210.

Chapter Seven

Beat the Bullies!

[Fight Unnecessary Insurance and Taxes]

They say the only two things you can count on are *death* and *taxes*! I think there's a third—*insurance hassles*! I can't do anything about the first one, but this chapter will help you lower your tax and insurance expenses.

Have things become more complicated the past ten years, or is it just me? It seems there are so many more things to keep track of when it comes to taxes and insurance, and especially for the retired couple who wants the highest quality retirement possible within a limited budget. Insurance salesmen are trying to convince us to buy speciality policies to protect us from every contingency, and we're being taxed on what we eat, drive, earn, sell, use or inherit. It's a wonder we have any money left to live on.

Let's start with insurance, and we might as well tackle the worst first—the health insurance fiasco!

Cut Health Insurance Costs

Retirees all over America are confused and entangled by the health insurance fiasco, and it's putting a real dent in their budgets. Straightening out a claim has the same headache rating as trying to do your own income taxes. More money is being thrown away needlessly because retirees don't know how to avoid the expensive pitfalls. Here's the best advice from experts that will help cut your costs:

When you retire try to retain your same group health insurance, even though you may need to pay for it out of your own pocket. This will usually give you a better rate, avoid a three to six month waiting period for new insurance to become effective, and prevent your needing to qualify for a new company's policy.

Don't purchase duplicate health insurance policies, whether a basic policy, major medical, catastrophic or other supplemental type policy. Unscrupulous salesmen from unscrupulous companies will try to sell you additional health coverage that you *don't need and can't afford*. They use scare tactics to get you to purchase a Medigap policy, for example, that you don't even need. Even after age sixty-five, when you're on Medicare Part A (free hospital coverage) or Part B (medical coverage, which is optional at about $29 a month), Medigap may not be the best way to go. Experts recommend a traditional health insurance plan to "stop the gaps" in your two Medicare plans. Nevertheless, you'll be bombarded by phone, door-to-door and especially direct mail to purchase these supplemental plans. The plans may sound real good, but the salesman may neglect to point out the fine print that says that the plan doesn't pay until "after sixty days in the hospital," or if you're "already in the hospital when you send in a claim," or if you haven't met the "elimination period," (which means they won't pay anything until you've been in the hospital one week). But, guess what? The average stay in the hospital is only one week, so you will have purchased a worthless policy. Another way they get you is with the "pre-existing illness exclusions," which means that you won't be paid for anything that relates to an illness you may have had before.

Order the Insurance Checklist for Life, Auto, Health and Residential *from* AARP.

The best advice is to avoid the scam artists, especially those using direct mail, no matter how much you love the actor giving the pitch on television. Fortunately, a new law went into effect in 1991 that will prevent a salesman from selling you one of these "stop-the-gap" policies if you already own one. So, be aware of what you have, and get rid of any duplicate policies.

A seventy-two-year-old grandma named Lil Simmons from Alexandria, Virginia, was recently used by the House Health Subcommittee of the Select Committee on Aging as an "undercover agent" to investigate the illegalities going on in the Medigap business. Using the home of a subcommittee staffer, Simmons met with twelve different agents in the District of Columbia, Virginia and Maryland. Always present was the staffer who had set up the appointment, pretending to be her niece or nephew. Although the subcommittee already knew Lil Simmons had adequate coverage, this is what the salesmen tried to do: Every agent except one said she needed additional coverage that exactly duplicated what she already had. In one instance, a new identical policy would have cost her 400 percent the premium she was already paying. One agent tried to dismiss her present health insurance policy as "worthless certificates" and suggested that life insurance would protect her much better. The agents used scare tactics such as "You're going to be a burden to your children in the years to come if you don't buy this policy."

This type of rip-off is taking place all over the country. You may think you won't fall for the "con," but it's amazing how convincing these salesmen can be. In Missouri, a seventy-year-old was sold twenty-seven health insurance policies,

These are the 1991 federal taxable income rates for married couples filing jointly:
0 to $34,000 income— 15 percent
$34,000 to $82,150—28 percent
Over $82,150—31 percent

and a widow bought twelve Medicare supplement policies from five different agents. Also, a couple in Texas bought six supplemental (Medigap) policies. Be careful that you aren't next!

When you turn sixty-five and are on Medicare, shop for a doctor who will accept you as a patient "on assignment." That means the doctor bills Medicare (you have no paperwork at all). The doctor agrees to charge you only the fee "approved" by Medicare. He'll get 80 percent of the fee paid to him by Medicare; you'll owe the other 20 percent, plus, of course, any part of the $75 a year deductible that Medicare charges. But if you've already satisfied this deductible for the year, for example, and the doctor bills Medicare $40 for his fee, you should only receive a bill for $8 (the 20 percent of the $40 fee).

On the other hand, if you go to a doctor who does not accept Medicare assignment, you must pay him his whole fee, then bill Medicare yourself, and eventually be reimbursed for 80 percent of *the Medicare approved amount*. Therefore, if a doctor charges $40, but the Medicare approved charge for the doctor's services is only $20, you'll be reimbursed 80 percent of

---

The Guide to Health Insurance for People with Medicare *(Publication No. HCFA-02110) is available from U.S. Dept. of Health & Human Services*

the $20, or $16, so you'll pay $24 cash from your pocket. Many doctors will accept assignment, and Medicare publishes a list of those in your area. They're called "Medicare Participating Physicians" and are on a list called "The Medicare Participating Physician/Supplier Directory," which is available through most local senior citizen organizations in your area. It's worth looking into because it will save you hundreds of dollars each year.

Beware of health insurance salesman who may try to convince you to "switch policies." By canceling your present policy and signing up for the new one, the salesman will get an up-front fee. Meanwhile, this may cause you great distress because, not only will you have new and additional paperwork, there will be a "waiting period" before you can make claims, often six months. What if you really need to make a claim before that time is up? Guess what? You pay! The salesman won't mention this at the time, however.

If, for some reason, you're in a situation where you must find a new carrier, shop carefully and wisely. Go to several of the A+ rated health insurance carriers and get prices and coverages from each; then make a chart in the privacy of your home where you can compare these companies' policies. Believe me—they are *not* all alike! There isn't a set price for a certain type of health insurance policy; there's great variation, so comparison shop. You'll need a good ba-

Nearly thirty million Americans over sixty-five elect to buy Medicare Part B supplementary insurance.

sic hospital/medical plan that covers as much as possible for the money. Then it will be up to you if you decide to supplement this policy with a "Major Medical" or a "Catastrophic" policy. The total monthly outlay for all these policies can run $300 a month per person, so be sure to shop for the best buys.

Joining a Health Maintenance Organization (HMO) may be a much less expensive way to go. Side benefits to going this route are the fact that you will never have any paperwork (even if you're on Medicare), and you won't have the extra expense of "Major Medical" or "Catastrophic" policies since an HMO has such complete hospital and medical coverage.

Examples of HMO's are the Kaiser/Permanente plan, Takecare, Lifeguard or Bay-Pacific HMO plan. You can choose from several wherever you live. There is some type of Kaiser plan available from Hawaii to Washington, D.C.

Just to give you an idea of how an HMO can save you money, here are some plans being offered by Kaiser/Permanente (as this book goes to press). If you're under sixty-five, they offer two plans:

• *$212.08 per month for a husband/wife. You pay $15 per doctor visit, $5 per lab test or Xray.*
• *$225.64 per month for a husband/wife. You pay $5 per doctor visit, $3 per lab test or Xray. Otherwise, all your hospital and medical is paid, except for prescrip-*

tion drugs, and there's no maximum number of days for your hospital stay.

If you're over sixty-five they offer one plan:

• *$119.16 per month for a husband/wife. You pay $3 per visit. No charge for any lab or Xrays. Prescriptions available at wholesale.*

> More Health for Your Dollar — an Older Person's Guide to HMO's *is available from AARP.*
>
>

Under this plan you must both be enrolled in Medicare Parts A and B, but Kaiser does all the paperwork; you never even get involved, much less pay any deductibles. By the way, if you're interested in a Kaiser HMO plan, call the Kaiser nearest you to see if you live in one of their service areas. You'll need to apply to join by filling out a form so that you can be screened. You'll be accepted based on your health, although they tell me the only way you would be denied is if you have a pre-existing, chronic life-threatening condition such as cancer.

My niece's father-in-law belongs to Kaiser and recently had triple bypass surgery; he was so pleased because all the expenses were paid—no forms to fill out—no hassle! This operation can run $50,000. Joining an HMO will save your precious retirement dollars in many ways: not only in your monthly premiums, but in your monthly out-of-pocket expenses. Then, as a bonus, you have no confusing paperwork that can make you sick in the first place!

If you've been in the military, look into any health benefits you have coming through the Veterans Administration. This will obviously save you thousands of dollars a year.

Don't be shy about applying for Medicaid (called Medi-cal in California), if you're eligible. This is in addition to Medicare, for which all seniors qualify automatically. Medicaid is additional insurance available to any of you whose income and assets may be extremely low. It can be a wonderful answer for your health insurance needs if you're among the three and a half million older Americans eligible for this godsend. It will pay your Medicare premiums, any co-payments and all deductibles. Call your local Social Security office to see if you qualify.

Cut Automobile Insurance Costs

The most obvious way to cut auto insurance costs is to drive a car that costs less to insure in the first place. Here are the cars with the lowest insurance rates in each of three price ranges:

Car Prices up to $10,000
Subaru Justy
Suzuki Swift
Toyota Tercel
Car Prices from $10,001 to $15,000
Dodge Caravan
Plymouth Voyager Turbo
Car Prices from $15,001 to $20,000
Dodge Grand Caravan
Ford LTD Wagon
Plymouth Grand Voyager NT
Volvo 240

If the new or used car you're thinking of purchasing isn't on this list, call several automobile insurance carriers to get their prices. You may decide to change your mind if the car you're dreaming of is in the high insurance cost category.

Here are some cars by price range that are the most expensive to insure:

Car Prices up to $10,000
Ford Escort GT
Mustang EX CONV
Hyundai Sonata
Nissan 2WD Pickup
VW GTI
VW Jetta
Car Prices from $10,001 to $15,000
Dodge Daytona Shelby
Geo Tracker
Mitsubishi Wagon
Nissan 240SX
Pontiac Firebird
Toyota Corolla
Car Prices from $15,001 to $20,000
Chevrolet Camaro
Nissan Pathfinder
Pontiac Firebird Trans Am
VW Cabriolet

Shop around for insurance; prices vary for the same coverage from company to company.

Save as much as 40 percent on your insurance by driving a car that has safety features such as air bags or automatic seat belts.

Save significantly on your premiums by agreeing to a higher deductible — particularly if you own a late-model car. The most popular deductible amount is $250, but people with good driving habits should consider going up to a $500 or even a $1,000 deductible.

Ask for discounts offered by the insurance companies; they may not always mention them to you. After all, the higher the premium, the more the salesman gets paid. Some discounts are available for being a non-smoker, a good driver, a non-drinker, and if you promise in writing that you and your passengers will always wear seatbelts.

Do without "Collision" coverage. This is the part of the policy that protects your car up to its market value. If it's an older car, you may be throwing your money away by carrying "Collision."

Beware of car rental agencies who try to pressure you into buying their CDW (Collision Damage Waiver) insurance. Legislation has recently been passed in a number of states eliminating the sale of CDWs. In California, a law was passed that limits the price of a CDW to $9 a day, but requires that the car rental company tell you that you're probably already covered on your own car insurance. Usually a CDW offers only limited protection and is a better deal for the rental company than for the motorist, but the main reason you may not need this type of insurance is that you're probably already covered through a credit card company or through your

---

Regarding quarterly Payment of Estimated Federal Taxes:

By law, you must pay the Internal Revenue Service 90 percent of your federal tax liability during the year to avoid penalty; however, you can escape this penalty if you're over sixty-two, have retired within the last two years, and have reasonable cause.

---

own car insurance. Call your insurance agent to see if a rental car is covered for collision on your policy before being coerced into buying one of these CDWs from a car rental company. This will save you from $9 to $17 a day.

Save on Your Life Insurance

The most common misconception about life insurance is that it's a permanent need that each family has. This is totally untrue! Life insurance is a way to buy time until you get your personal financial estate in order, so you need more coverage when you're young and less when you're older. A more scientific name for this is "The Theory of Decreasing Responsibility." As you get older, your responsibilities decrease—children are grown and on their own, routine payments are reduced, your home is probably paid for. This is the time of your life when you can save insurance dollars by dropping some of this excess.

Another thing you may want to consider is converting your term insurance to whole life because your term insurance premiums will just soar as you grow older, but by converting them to whole life, your premiums will remain constant, and the amount that builds up in the investment portion will pay off the policy.

Many new, innovative insurance products have been developed in the last few years. You may want to drop outdated products entirely or replace with a new type of policy that will give you more protection for less cost. To give you an idea of what I mean by "outdated," many old policies discriminated between men and women, forcing men or women to pay higher premiums. Many new policies don't differentiate. Another characteristic of old policies was the required health examination; many new policies aren't based on your health. Also, many old policies required that you pay on them until your death. Today, new policies let you pay for only fifteen years, and then you may withdraw all the money you paid in. This can be especially helpful if you're seventy-five, for example, when you may need the cash for health care costs more than you need protection for your family in case of your death. Talk to your insurance agent and see if there may be a new-style policy that appeals to you.

Stay away from fancy options on insurance policies. Don't load up on gimmicks such as "option to purchase additional insurance," "accidental death rider," "mortgage insurance rider."

Avoid "credit life" policies of any kind, such as the type you're pressured to purchase when you buy a car or other major item. Credit life is nothing more than a very expensive form of decreasing term insurance.

If you're a veteran, you should be aware that you can have free burial in a national cemetery, a fact that one-third of the nation's twenty-seven million living veterans don't realize. The Veterans Administration presently buries about 10 percent of all veterans. Be aware of this free benefit as you plan your life insurance needs.

The average annual homeowner's insurance policy cost $394 in 1991.

Save on Homeowner's or Renter's Insurance

Review your homeowner's insurance; be sure you aren't over-insured. One common mistake is that the insurance covers the estimated market value of the total property, rather than the house and contents themselves. The value of the land should be subtracted from the whole, so that you're insuring the structures themselves, because land can't burn. Another mistake is made when a policy is padded with unneeded "gimmicky extras" such as riders on your furs and jewelry. You may want to reevaluate the replacement cost of any furs to see if it's really worth the extra insurance expense. Also, you may want to consider placing valuable jewelry or family heirlooms in your safety deposit box, so that you don't need to carry special insurance on these items either. Try to cut the cost of your policy down as much as possible while maintaining the essential coverage.

Some insurance companies will cut the cost of homeowner's or mobile home insurance policies if you've installed deadbolt locks, fire extinguishers, smoke alarms and other safety features.

Look into the cost of installing these items. It may be worth it for the money you'll save on your policy and the comfort you'll get from these safety features.

When purchasing renter's insurance, be careful that you don't accidentally buy a policy that duplicates what the landlord already has in place. Call your landlord to discuss his policy. You may find that you can get by with minimum renter's insurance coverage.

Always shop around for insurance because there's a big variation in prices for the same coverage. Don't be shy about calling five companies in one day asking for their rates.

There is a coalition of life, health and property insurance groups that offer a toll-free insurance helpline. If you have questions about any of your insurance needs, call (800)942-4242.

Lower Your State and Federal Income Taxes

Everyone wants to pay as little tax as legally possible, but this is especially important for the retiree on a small budget. We retired people have better things to spend our money on—travel, golf lessons, a new transmission for our one and only car. So, let's look at ways to keep our cash at home.

If you have a choice of a state in which to retire, you may want to select one that has little or no personal income tax. Alaska, Florida, Nevada, South Dakota, Texas, Washington and Wyoming have no personal income tax at all. New Hampshire and Tennessee tax only income from dividends and interest, and

Connecticut taxes only capital gains and dividends.

These states do not tax Social Security benefits at all:

Alabama	Maryland
Arizona	Massachusetts
Arkansas	Michigan
California	Mississippi
Delaware	New Jersey
Georgia	New Mexico
Hawaii	New York
Idaho	North Carolina
Illinois	Oklahoma
Indiana	Oregon
Kentucky	Pennsylvania
Louisiana	South Carolina
Maine	Virginia

Each state has its own taxation on federal civil service pensions, military employee pensions, state and local government pensions, and private employer pensions. Each state also has its own personal exemption allowances for older taxpayers. An excellent reference book that tells exactly what income each state taxes is *Retirement Places Rated*. Another publication that will help you is called *Relocation Tax Guide: State Tax Information for Relocation Decisions, (D13400)*, available from AARP Fulfillment (EE175).

When it comes to federal income taxes, it doesn't matter which state you live in—residents of all states are taxed the same. However, the best ways to cut your federal taxes are to:

1. Get professional advice.
2. Be sure to take every single deduction possible.

You may already have someone who helps you with your taxes. If not, here are some sources of free tax advice:

"Walk-in service" available through the IRS. Although they won't actually prepare your tax returns for you, they'll "walk you through it" so you can prepare your own return. This is usually done in a group setting. Just show up at any IRS office and go to the "Walk-in Counter."

The Volunteer Income Tax Assistance program (VITA) provides free tax assistance to senior citizens. Check with your senior center to find their locations.

Tax Counseling for the Elderly (TCE) also provides free tax assistance to people over sixty. Both VITA and TCE sites are usually located in neighborhood senior centers, at libraries, at churches or at other places in the community.

The next thing you can do to save money on your federal income tax is to take every deduction coming to you. There are many good books out on this subject, most available for free at your local library, but these are some of the most common mistakes made by retirees:

According to Money magazine, the four most heavily taxed places to live are Washington, D.C., New York, Massachusetts and Wisconsin.

• *They don't take the "additional exemption" that is available to those sixty-five or older.*
• *They accidentally list interest income from municipal bonds that are tax exempt.*
• *They accidentally list all their Social Security benefits as income; only part of it is taxable on your federal return.*
• *They don't realize that they can deduct a "Capital Loss" on stock losses.*
• *If the retiree runs a small business out of his home, he may neglect to take all the deductions coming to him such as a portion of his health insurance premiums, depreciation on office equipment, mileage or auto expenses, a percentage of home costs (utilities, insurance, taxes, depreciation, mortgage interest), postage, etc.*
• *They don't keep accurate records of their medical and dental expenses that can be deducted, including 9 cents per mile to and from medical/dental offices.*
• *They don't list losses from fire, theft or accident.*
• *They don't realize they may be able to deduct their total moving expenses.*
• *They don't realize they may be able to take a onetime $125,000 exclusion when they sell their home.*
• *They don't deduct a penalty for early withdrawal from a time savings account.*
• *They fail to file quarterly statements for estimated tax with the IRS, if necessary, which eliminates paying a penalty at the end of the year.*
• *They fail to deduct charitable contributions of non-cash items such as clothing or merchandise. An appraisal can be made when these items are donated, the amount of which can be deducted on your income tax.*

Money Magazine recently told of a Boston retiree and his wife who have managed to pay no federal income tax for the past four years. Here's how they do it:

(Tax-free income)	
• *Tax-exempt interest from muni bonds*	*$6,059*
• *Social Security benefits*	*13,910*
• *Total tax-free income*	*19,969*
(Taxable income)	
• *Taxable interest*	*2,328.*
• *Dividend income*	*10*
• *Capital gain*	*1,541*
• *Taxable IRA and other pension distributions*	*5,974*
• *Adjusted gross income*	*9,853*
• *Itemized Deductions*	*0*
• *Standard deduction (married, filing jointly)*	*-5,000*
• *65-or-older deduction (filer and spouse)*	*-1,200*
• *Balance of taxable income*	*3,653*
• *Personal exemptions (2)*	*-3,800*
• *Amount of tax owed*	*0*

This retiree says he really enjoys not paying the government more in taxes than he has to. He says he has never been audited, but if it ever happens, he can defend every number on his returns. He also is a great believer in the wisdom of Judge Learned Hand who wrote in a 1934 decision:

"Anyone may so arrange his affairs that his taxes shall be as low as possible; he is not bound to choose that pattern which will best pay the Treasury; there is not even a patriotic duty to increase one's taxes."

So, go for it, fellow retiree! If it's legal, deduct it, and keep your cash for fun stuff!

Save on State Sales Tax

If you have a choice of state in which to retire, you may want to choose one of these that charges no sales tax at all: Alaska, Delaware, Montana, New Hampshire, Oregon.

Purchase things at flea markets, garage sales and through classified ads in the newspapers where the sellers must work out their own payment of sales taxes, which never seem to be "added on" to the price you pay for an item.

If you live in a state that charges sales tax, but you aren't that far from a state that doesn't, it may be worth the time and trouble to purchase big ticket items from the other state. We live in California but many people we know drive to Oregon to purchase goods. One man flies there every other year or so, buys a car, and drives it home. Six percent of $15,000 is $900, enough to pay for unlimited golf for him and his wife for one year.

Most of the retirees I interviewed were very concerned about their total tax burden. Some had already caught on that no sales tax is charged on items at flea markets, garage sales or in classified ads. Many others were tuned in to the tax savings of tax-free investments, which we'll discuss more in Chapter Eleven.

I don't have a cure for all your headaches, but I hope I've helped eliminate any that are insurance or tax related.

"Take this chapter and call me in the morning!"

Chapter Eight

Here's to Your Health!

[Keep Your Medical Costs Down]

Now that you're retired and have your best years ahead of you, you want them to be healthy! Every morning when you wake up you want to feel like Gordon MacRae as he sang "Oh, What a Beautiful Morning," in *Oklahoma*. In this chapter, we'll look at all the ways to prevent health problems so that every morning will be beautiful, and when you do have that occasional health expense, we'll look at the many ways they can be lowered.

What do retired Americans usually pay for their total health costs? According to the U.S. Senate Special Committee on Aging, these are the percentages of income spent on health care by age groups:

Under 65	*5%*
65-74 years of age	*9%*
75 and older	*12.5%*

Unfortunately, the retirees represented in these statistics haven't read this book, but all you lucky readers will be able

> *The average American gets 40 to 45 percent of his daily calories from fat. The American Heart Association recommends no more than 30 percent.*

to lower these percentages if you follow the advice of the experts.

Eat Nutritionally Balanced Meals

As we already discovered in Chapter Five, it's important to eat healthy foods, not only to maintain proper weight, but also to have a healthy heart, strong bones and even a resistance to disease.

Dr. Kenneth G. Manton, professor and assistant director of Duke University's Center for Demographic Studies says, ". . . proper nutrition and exercise . . . can do a great deal to reduce risks of early death due to cardiovascular disease or cancer." Dr. Manton also states that his recent study proved that it's even more important to adopt healthy habits as we age because the body gradually becomes less capable of tolerating abuse.

According to Dr. Curtis Mettlin, Director of Cancer Control at the Roswell Park Memorial Institute in Buffalo, New York, we should all be eating more cabbage-family vegetables such as cauliflower, broccoli and brussels sprouts, and Henry T. Lynch, a researcher at the Creighton University School of Medicine, says that scientists can say for sure now that a high-fiber, low-fat diet is a "prudent" precaution against cancer.

Dr. Lynch also says that once cancer has developed, there has been no reputable research that shows that special diets or food supplements can effectively defeat the disease.

Cancer has to be the most dreaded disease for all of us. It probably cannot be treated by diet after we already have it, but it may be prevented by proper diet beforehand, so why don't we all give nutrition a chance?

I spoke with a representative at the National Cancer Institute who said some studies indicate that eating certain vegetables (carrots, broccoli and cabbage) may be helpful in preventing cancer. They have a great little booklet out called *Eat More Fruits and Vegetables*, which they will send to you if you call them at their toll-free number, (800)4-CANCER. If you're not fond of the vegetables I mentioned above, this booklet will give you some other choices.

There are hundreds of studies that prove that healthful eating can relieve, prevent or reverse many of today's worst killer diseases such as stroke, osteoporosis, diabetes, high cholesterol, high blood pressure or heart disease. The Rodale Food and Nutrition Research Center in Emmaus, Pennsylvania, has come up with a cookbook called *Prevention's Meals That Heal Cookbook* that will help you eat foods that prevent diseases. You can order it by writing Rodale Books, Box 8, Emmaus, PA 18099-0008. While you're at it, why not subscribe to *Prevention Magazine*, too? It will update you with all kinds of nutrition news to keep you healthy. And not only will good nutrition keep you healthy so your retirement years are the most fun, but you'll cut down on your total health care costs!

If you have any questions on nutrition, call the Nutrition Hotline sponsored by the American Institute for Cancer Research (800)843-8114. Weight Watchers has also produced a booklet titled *Healthy Living for Life*, which will not only give you good nutritional advice, but will also help if you're overweight. For a free copy, call (800)726-6108.

> *Scientists say exercise creates a feeling of well-being and mental alertness. It relieves stress and improves your ability to manage problems.*

Exercise!

Please don't throw this book across the room—I know you've heard this several thousand times, and you're sick of hearing it! I can sure understand that, but just look at the facts. A recent survey shows that 59 percent of Americans are "couch potatoes"; however, the Centers for Disease Control in Atlanta says that "inactivity is the most widespread of all preventable heart attack risks." Also, the *Journal of the American Medical Association* says that one of the largest studies of its kind provides strong new evidence that physically fit people live longer and that even moderate exercise, such as brisk walking, could result in much lower death rates from heart disease and cancer. Dr. Steven Blair, the lead author of this study, said, "The important public health message is that moderate levels of fitness seem to offer benefit, or protection, from early death."

Who doesn't want "protection from early death"? Of course, everyone wants it, but how many of you out there are willing to lift your "potato off the couch" and *at least* go for a thirty to forty-five minute walk several days a week? If you hate walking alone, join a mall or outdoor walking club. There's one in your town, I'm sure. In Atlanta, Georgia, for example, there are more than one hundred senior citizen walking clubs; they even have names, like the "High Milers," "High Steppers," and the "Walky Talkies."

Those who walk the malls like the shelter and safety of indoors. Personally, I love to be out in the elements, even if it's a warm or cool day; the fresh air seems to lift my spirits.

In any case, be sure to check with your doctor before starting any exercise program, and if you prefer swimming, bicycling, or aerobics, try them out. Tennis and golf can be a lot of fun, too, even though they aren't "aerobic," they're better than sitting!

Remember that exercise bike you bought once at a garage sale? Drag it from under the tarp on your patio, clean it up, and stick it in front of your TV. You'll go from "couch potato" to "bicycle banana" in no time, and you'll find that your health

will improve and your medical bills will go down.

Butt Out!

I know most of you out there who smoke really would like to quit if you could, and I know the reasons you haven't been able to do it. According to the Hope Heart Institute in Seattle, smokers give these reasons for smoking:

• *"The nicotine in cigarettes gives me a lift and keeps me going."*
• *"It's relaxing—it keeps me from feeling anxious."*
• *"Smoking helps me cope with difficult people and problems."*
• *"I'm hooked on nicotine."*
• *"It's just a habit."*

In response, health experts offer these observations:

• *Brief periods of exercise and plenty of rest can provide the same lift—without guilt.*
• *The "relaxation" you feel when you smoke is actually the easing of nicotine withdrawal symptoms. Kicking an addiction to nicotine is the* long-term *key to relaxation.*
• *For alternative ways to deal with stress, try brisk exercise, a warm shower, or slow, deep breathing.*
• *The best way to beat nicotine withdrawal symptoms is to quit smoking—suddenly and completely. Drink lots of water to help flush the nicotine from your system and cut down on caffeinated drinks to minimize the jitters. Reach for a snack of fresh fruit, sugarless*

gum or candy when you get the urge to smoke.

• *To break the habit, try to become more aware of each cigarette you smoke. You can do this by smoking with the opposite hand.*

There are obviously many more important reasons to quit smoking than just cutting down on your health costs; after all, you'll live longer and feel better for the rest of your life. You'll also cut your risks of lung cancer, pulmonary disease and, of course, heart disease. But, you must admit the financial rewards are pretty enticing. The very fact that you won't be buying a carton of cigarettes every time you go to the store should be pretty motivating! By the way, take some of that money and reward yourself, because if you can quit smoking, you deserve it!

The experts say that your greatest chance of success in quitting smoking is to consult a professional, either your personal doctor, or by going through the program at your local hospital. Another source of help to any of you who want to quit smoking is to call the American Cancer Society toll-free at (800)227-2345.

It is reported that 85 percent of all lung cancers have been caused by smoking.

sults of studies were being published that prove that an aspirin a day becomes a "clot buster," thus preventing heart attacks for many. In 1985, after reviewing seven studies, federal health officials announced that taking one aspirin (about 325 milligrams) a day could help some heart attack victims reduce the likelihood of a second attack. Recently, another study found that even among healthy male physicians who had not suffered heart attacks, taking aspirin made it much less likely they would fall prey to a heart attack than another similar group that did not take aspirin.

Ask your doctor before starting aspirin therapy, but it may be a way to stay healthy and therefore reduce your total health costs.

Make Friends

This may sound like a funny way to cut down on your medical costs, but scientists have found that there is such a thing as *social healing* that can take place caused by the effects of human-to-human bonds, also known as social ties. Scientists say that these social ties are related to lower rates of disease and death. People need loving relationships — good friends they can talk to. Just having someone to confide in can prevent you from internalizing stress and worry, thus preventing illness and disease. Isn't that good news? So, go out and make a friend, particularly if you've just moved into a new retirement environ-

Take an Aspirin a Day

I used to think this was some kind of "quack" advice until our own doctor recommended it, and at the same time re-ment. Don't be shy—it's for your own good, and the good of your pocketbook!

Get a Physical Exam Once a Year

Don't wait until you're sick to go to the doctor. So many of us hate going in for a checkup because we're afraid the doctor will find something wrong. Listen, that's really foolish because statistics show that most of the life-threatening diseases can be halted if caught in time.

The purpose of an annual pap smear, rectal exam, prostate check or mammogram is to catch cancer at its earliest possible stage, when it's still treatable!

It's also smart to have a complete blood test once a year; it reveals imbalances in your blood sugar, cholesterol count, and dozens of other signs that will give your doctor a chance to prolong your life. Adding years to your life and staying healthy are the most important reasons to have annual checkups, but, let's face it, look at the money you'll save in the *big bills* that could come along if you don't!

Get Your Flu Shots

Dr. Walter Gunn, an epidemiologist with the government's Centers for Disease Control in Atlanta says, "Of the twenty thousand persons a year who die of flu, at least 90 percent are sixty-five or older." Another expert, Dr. Robert Webster of St. Jude's Children's Research Hospital in Memphis, says, "While a bout of influenza is miserable for most of us, it can be serious or even fatal for people over sixty-five."

Experts say that even if the flu vaccine doesn't prevent flu for you, it will greatly reduce the severity and complications of the disease.

Check with your doctor to see if he or she recommends a flu shot for you each year, and, if so, do it! A little pain today will prevent a big one later on, not to say anything of the one you'll feel in your pocketbook!

Get a Pet

Did you know that research has provided overwhelming evidence that people who own dogs and cats are healthier than those without pets. Dr. Judith Siegel, a psychologist at UCLA who studied Medicare records of an HMO for a *New Choices* magazine article, found that pet owners made far fewer visits to their doctors than did folks without pets. Dr. Siegel says that pets help humans handle stress by providing companionship, security, and feelings of being loved and needed.

So, how about a trip to your local Humane Society? Or contact: Purina Pets for People, Checkerboard Square, 6T, St. Louis, MO 63164. They'll work through your local humane society to provide pets for free to anyone sixty or older. There's no initial cost to the retiree; all adoption fees, initial vet visits, spaying or neutering are paid by Purina.

Beware of the Con Artist

We have talked about the con artist in other chapters, but he's really out to get you when it comes to medical scams. Usually these scams are presented with the words "miracle" or "secret cure" or "scientific breakthrough."

There are thousands of dishonest salesmen and "quacks" who know that senior citizens are vulnerable prospects. How do you tell if you're getting suckered? The first clue may be the practitioners' diagnostic methods. According to the American Council on Science and Health beware of:

Applied Kinesiology. By pushing down, in or up on a person's extremities, the practitioner claims to be able to diagnose diseases and nutritional deficiencies. This test has failed scientific evaluations, however.

Iridology. Proponents say the eye's iris reveals pathological, structural and functional disturbances in the body. Scientific studies have failed to confirm the efficacy of it.

Hair Analysis. For this test, about two tablespoons of hair are clipped from the nape of the neck and sent to a commercial "hair analysis lab." The lab sends back a list of the excesses and recommended nutritional supplements. Since levels of nutrients in the hair don't reflect levels in the body, lab analyses make important errors.

Live Cell Analysis. The cells in a drop of blood are examined by a "special microscopic technique" called dark-field microscopy, through which proponents say they can see nutritional deficiencies and other diseases. To scientists, it's like gypsies reading tea leaves.

Some mobile medical labs that offer free diagnostic exams to older Americans may be nothing more than scam operations out to bilk Medicare, according to

AARP. Unscrupulous lab operators may claim that the free tests have uncovered medical problems that require costly additional tests, for which Medicare is billed thousands of dollars. Patients rarely get the test results, so genuinely ill persons aren't alerted.

Quacks who try to convince people they can eat all they want and still lose weight. In fact, they even say you can lose weight while you're sleeping. Don't be caught by these cons!

Obviously, entire books could be written on medical scams; however, the United States Office of Consumer Affairs gives this advice:

• *Check with your doctor, pharmacist or other health professional before buying health care products or programs. For instance, medical science has not yet found a cure for arthritis, so products that promise to cure you of the disease are extremely suspect.*
• *Be aware that fraudulent health care products can rob you of more than money. They can steal your health and even your life by causing you to delay appropriate health care.*

Top Twenty Ways to Save on Medical Costs

Let's face it, even if you do take an aspirin a day, get a pet, stop smoking, diet, exercise, get your flu shot, and confide in a friend, you're going to need professional medical care eventually. You can't prevent everything, right? Here are the best ways to cut those inevitable costs that we all must face eventually:

Cut your health insurance costs every way possible, as discussed in Chapter Seven.

If you're sixty-five and on Medicare, shop for a doctor who will "take you on assignment." As we also discussed in the previous chapter, this can save you 40 percent on your bill.

Save on all your medical, hospital and pharmacy costs by joining an HMO where your doctor's visits can run $5 to $15 and your lab tests $3 to $5. Prescription drugs are sometimes available at $5 each or at wholesale. These plans vary, so check them out.

If you can get health benefits from past military service, take advantage of them. Call your local Veterans Administration office, or contact Veterans Health Services (address and phone in Appendix A).

Take advantage of Medicaid. Don't be shy about calling your local Social Security office to see if you're eligible.

Take advantage of free or discounted vision and dental care through colleges and universities that accept patients through their degree programs. Excellent care is available through these sources such as dental care through the University of California, San Francisco. All work is done by students, but supervised by the instructors, so you can be sure the work will be done right.

Accept free cholesterol testing or other medical testing through *legitimate*

> *It is estimated that Medicare pays about 48.8 percent of all medical costs for those over sixty-five.*

agencies such as hospitals, an employer, American Red Cross or other health organization.

Always ask for discounts that are available to senior citizens from your doctor, dentist or pharmacy.

If your prescriptions are not covered by insurance, always ask for the generic equivalent of any drug when having your prescription filled, or buy an over-the-counter equivalent, which will be even less expensive. A drug store's own brand of ibuprofen, for example, may be the same as a prescribed equivalent. (Ask your doctor or pharmacist to advise you on this; don't make the substitution on your own because strengths differ.) You can also send your prescriptions to discount mail-order pharmacies that are recommended by legitimate sources such as AARP. One highly recommended mail-order pharmacy is The Drug Emporium, at 7792 Olentangy River Road, Worthington, OH 43085; (614)846-2511.

If your prescriptions are covered by insurance, ask your doctor for prescriptions to cover any over-the-counter drugs you have been buying for hay fever, colds, pain relief, etc. I recommend you read an excellent book on this whole subject of drugs; you can get it free at your local library: *Complete Guide to Prescription and Non-Prescription Drugs* by H. Winter Griffith, M.D.

Use home remedies for anything that is safe to do so. For example, many doctors recommend that women drink cranberry juice for bladder infections, and one home remedy guide suggests using ordinary baking soda to stop athlete's foot. A good source of home remedies is called *The Doctor's Book of Home Remedies* by the editors of Prevention Magazine Health Books available through Rodale Books. See Appendix A for address.

Prevent cavities by brushing twice a day and flossing once a day with the "horseshoe method." This is not the same as merely slipping a piece of dental floss between each tooth, which only removes chunks of food. Make a loop of the dental floss and rub it up and down against the inside of each tooth to "rub away the sticky bacteria." If you can picture it, you would be using your dental floss *twice* between each space between two teeth — first you rub the dental floss against the one tooth, and then against the other. Ask your dentist or dental hygienist to show you how to do this; it's very easy and can actually prevent cavities from starting.

Call your pharmacist when you have a minor health problem, rather than making an appointment with your medical doctor right away. Very often the pharmacist can recommend an over-the-counter drug that may alleviate the problem. If that doesn't work, you can go to your doctor. At least you'll have given it a try.

Order Diet, Nutrition and Cancer Prevention; The Good News *from the National Cancer Institute,* (800)4-CANCER.

If you have your choice of hospitals, select a voluntary, nonprofit, teaching hospital accredited by the Joint Commission on Accreditation of Hospitals (address in Appendix A). This assures you of a hospital that conforms to basic standards in its operation and in the delivery of care and services and will give you the highest level of care at the lowest possible cost.

Don't be admitted to a hospital on a Friday, Saturday, Sunday or holiday if you have a choice, because most routine testing services operate only from Monday through Friday afternoon and you might be forced to stay an extra unnecessary day to wait for these services.

Always ask your doctor if "Same-Day-Surgery" is possible. This cuts costs considerably for minor operations such as urinary-tract surgery, D&C, cyst removals, hernia operations, etc.

When hospitalized, always accept a semiprivate room, if that is all that's covered on your insurance.

Always ask for a second opinion when surgery is recommended. Many insurance companies require a second opinion anyway; if yours doesn't, take charge and ask for it.

Question whether prescribed medical tests are really necessary and whether two tests may duplicate each other in results received. You may discover, just by asking a simple question, that two or more tests *don't* need to be done the same day, but can wait until the results of the first one are available, which may mean that no more tests are needed. **When having your eyes or hearing tested,** always shop around for the best deal, which is to have them checked as a package deal. You'll get your glasses or hearing aid at the same place you have your examination, thus saving money. Don't go to an eye doctor for an exam and then take your prescription somewhere else to be filled. Try for the "one-price-quote" so you won't have any expensive surprises.

I asked all those retirees I interviewed what they do to cut down on their medical costs. Here are some of their replies:

• *"I use good hygiene and eating habits."*
• *"We go to the doctor only when absolutely necessary, and we use generic drugs."*
• *"We refrain from smoking and drinking; eat moderately; take daily walks."*
• *"I buy plastic lens glasses at $39.95 a pair and stay clear of people with colds, flu, etc."*

• *"I take good care of my teeth—floss and brush two times a day, and I eat right."*
• *"We find doctors who accept Medicare assignment."*

If you've always been couch potatoes who loved to smoke, eat pizza, and never cared much for exercise, I hope this chapter has helped you see the importance of making changes in your life. These changes will not only help you live longer and feel better, but they'll also prevent expensive medical costs that may come your way during retirement.

When you do need to seek medical help, use the twenty moneysaving suggestions, and you may be able to cut your total medical costs below the national average.

Take all the money you'll save on your medical costs and spend it on fun stuff, like leisure activities and little trips; we'll cover these subjects in the next couple chapters but, believe me, bowling and beaches are a lot more fun than bedpans and blood tests!

Chapter Nine

Have the Time of Your Life!

[Quality Leisure Time on a Tight Budget]

"I'm too busy to help; I just don't have enough time." This is a common statement made by all of us before retirement. We really don't have enough time to do all the things we're asked to do, much less all the things we need to do.

"I'm bored; I have too much time on my hands." Would you believe this is what many say after they've retired?

What causes this change? Wouldn't you think that the retirement years would be the most fun and fulfilling of your life? They should be and can be; however, many retirees get caught in a trap. You see, when they stopped working, they gave up a form of fulfillment and accomplishment, including contact with other people. They no longer needed to set their alarms, get up, and rush to work in the commuter traffic. Suddenly, they have all day with "nothing to do." What happened to all those things you said you would do when you retired? They're pushed to the back of your minds and a lethargy sets in that can become paralyzing unless you recog-

Doug Henderson, fifty-nine, won his age division of the Cape Cod Endurance Triathlon, and qualified for the Iron Man World Championship in Hawaii.

nize the problem and do something about it.

On the other hand, there are many retirees who always dreamed of traveling to exotic places, restoring an antique car, or buying a winter home in the desert, but when they realize their budgets are smaller than expected, they just sit and sour. What all of these retirees need is to *get involved*! There are literally thousands of hobbies, sports, classes, trips and volunteer jobs ready to fill your hours, and, fortunately, most require very little financial outlay on your part. Let's look at some of your opportunities. I've divided these opportunities into three categories: Playing, Learning and Helping.

Playing

Sports

Golf. If you love golf, now you have all the precious time you need to enjoy the game. Remember how frustrating it used to be to squeeze in a round of golf between work, home and family commitments? To enjoy unlimited golf on a budget, you can play at a public course; for a yearly or monthly fee you can play all the golf you want. Many of these fees run from $200 a year to $100 a month for a couple. If you've reached a certain age (sixty or sixty-five), you'll probably receive a discount on top of that. If you've moved to a retirement community that offers golf, your golf may be included in your monthly dues.

Tennis. There are public tennis courts where you can play for free, or for 25 cents an hour for a lighted court. Tennis is one of the least expensive sports you can take up, and if you decide to join a tennis club, some are priced very reasonably.

Bowling. Call around for senior rates, and you'll find that you can afford to bowl three or four times a week, particularly if you can play during the day on weekdays. Remember when you were working, and you had to schedule everything into a couple of free evenings a week? Now you have a wide open calendar and can pick up on the good daytime rates.

Skiing. If you love to ski, but must do so on a small budget, you'll probably find that cross-country skiing is the best idea. The price is right — it's free! Also, the equipment is very inexpensive compared to downhill. The actual exercise from cross-country skiing is much more healthful, too, because it's aerobic. I lived in Colorado for sixteen years and went from

A recent survey by the Marriott Corporation shows that hobbies, reading, sports recreation, and watching TV are the top activities of retired people.

downhill to cross-country after about ten. I found that downhill had become way too costly ($30 for a lift ticket), the lift lines were long, the equipment was expensive, the traffic was awful, and I was cold most of the time because of so much standing around. When I took up cross-country skiing a whole new world opened up to me. It's much more peaceful and invigorating, as well as affordable. Also, there are usually never any traffic snarls when driving to cross-country trails. Another unexpected pleasure that comes as a fringe benefit of cross-country skiing is the "lunch in the snow." You wear a lightweight day pack filled with cheese, crackers, fruit, a little Zinfandel, and chocolate treats for dessert, and take a big trash bag with you. When you're ready for your lunch, use the trash bag to sit on and enjoy. When you're finished eating, use the trash bag to discard your garbage. So, the trash bag serves as a waterproof blanket, a tablecloth and garbage sack — ingenious! I highly recommend this sport, and I guarantee you two things: You'll not only save a lot of money, but your health will improve as well.

Ice skating. Once you buy your very own pair of ice skates, many mountain resort communities provide free ice skating, and some city rinks offer senior discounts. When we lived in Colorado our whole family used to skate at the Keystone ice rink. The ice rink was lighted at night, there was music playing, and best of all, it didn't cost anything.

Swimming. Here's a great aerobic sport for you! Swim on senior rates at your public pool. Find a time when most children are in school and lap swimming is available. Time yourself to see how long it takes you to swim one lap and then set goals so that each time you swim you improve your time. Pretty soon you'll be swimming a third of a mile in half an hour, and you'll feel really proud! Usually monthly or seasonal rates are available such as $30 for a three-month period. That fits right into your budget, doesn't it? And if your town doesn't have an enclosed pool in the winter, and it's too cold to swim outdoors, call local motels and hotels for non-guest rates. My mother swims three times a week at a Howard Johnsons in Dublin, California, for $2 a swim. The pool is covered and usually deserted when she goes to swim at noon and guests haven't yet checked in for the evening. Your doctor will be so proud of you if you tell him you're swimming three days a week, and the side benefits will be sound sleep and high spirits.

If you've moved to a retirement community or senior apartment complex, you'll probably have all the swimming you want for free, and you sure can't beat that!

City league competitive sports. There are so many things to choose from—baseball and softball leagues, basketball, volleyball, 5 and 10 K races, and on and on. You don't need to compete with the twenty-five-year-olds either because they have leagues available for your age group. You'll not only have a lot of fun, improve your health, and stay within your "leisure activity budget," but you'll make some great friends, too.

Informal games. There are many competitive adult games to play, too, such as ping pong, billiards, shuffleboard, horseshoes, etc. Get involved! All these things are free so you have no excuses!

Bicycling. We already discussed this great sport, and it's certainly inexpensive to pursue. Bike clubs for seniors are really fun, and all you need is a good-quality bicycle, a helmet and comfortable biking attire.

Dancing. There are all kinds of dance clubs from square dancing to Texas two-step to ballroom. If you enjoy competing, there are also contests you can enter that are really exciting!

Clubs

Needless to say, there are hundreds of worthwhile clubs you can join. Before retirement you didn't have the time needed for the commitment it takes to be a faithful, productive club member, but you have gobs of time now, right? So, pick one or two clubs to visit; try them out, and if they appeal to you, consider joining. There are clubs for every personality type. If you're the shy type, find a club with a purpose where you can contribute in a quiet way. If you're more outgoing, you may want to join a social group like one in my area called the "Manteca Sunshine

Forever Young Dance Club: 8:00 P.M., second Saturday at the Senior Citizen Center. Your $3 admission charge includes refreshments and live music. This was a recent ad found on the "Over Fifty" page in a Modesto, California newspaper.

Seniors" that has potlucks, socials and dances, or how about joining a barbershop club?

There are the "Sweet Adelines" for women or the "Society for the Preservation and Encouragement of Barber Shop Quartet Singing in America" for men. Both of these groups can use your voice, and you'll never have so much fun! Every rehearsal is a riot, and the competitions are spine tingling. In fact, if your group wins a local or regional competition, you progress to nationals.

There are public speaking clubs such as "Toastmasters," and service clubs such as the American Business Women's Association that conducts fund-raisers to create scholarships for needy students. There are bridge and chess clubs, too, which can really challenge your brain and give you something to study up on between meetings! If you want something inexpensive, yet fulfilling, to do, consider a club.

Hobbies

Painting. You always wanted to try watercolors, right? Any type of painting, whether it's with oil, acrylics or any other medium, takes lots of time, just what you happen to have plenty of these days! My favorite is tole painting because it lends itself to inexpensive gift-giving. Tole painting is that old-fashioned country folk art that you see on antiques or rustic pieces of wood. Some of the patterns might be simple fruits or detailed scenes of home and family. You can tole paint on items you buy cheap at garage sales, or on things you already have around the house. The lessons are reasonable, too, and you'll never lose interest. After six les-

sons I could paint daisies, leaves, apples, pears, peaches and strawberries. It's great fun!

Cooking. Here is another hobby that's very time-consuming, and you never really got "with it" when you were working. Why not take a few cooking classes? Many are available free through your County Department of Home Economics or on television. Take classes that require inexpensive, available foodstuffs such as zucchini, which you may happen to have growing in your garden, or fruits or breads. Stay away from the foreign foods that require the expensive spices and wines. While you're at it, learn to cook fat-free! Not only is cooking a healthy hobby, but a moneysaving one if it keeps you out of restaurants!

Crafts. There are dozens of craft ideas that can be pursued on a small budget such as making "bottle dolls," wooden mobiles, Christmas tree ornaments, handmade paper kites, etc. An all-inclusive list would be as thick as Webster's dictionary, but you get the idea. The key is to use craft ideas that require inexpensive materials, and, while you're at it, why not make things that can be given later as birthday or Christmas gifts? That way you are saving money two ways.

Sewing. Shop carefully for your fabrics and materials so that you keep your sewing projects within your limited budget, and don't ignore free fabric available in garage sale clothing.

I've purchased out-of-style dresses, particularly floor length, that have yards and yards of excellent fabric within the skirts. These dresses are usually so out of date they don't sell, and if you stop by during the last few minutes of the sale, you can pick them up for 10 or 25 cents a piece. This trick will not only keep you stocked in plenty of fabric for your throw pillows or grandchildren's overalls or jackets, but you'll have plenty of zippers and buttons thrown in for free.

Gardening. Ah, here's something! Now you can indulge! Take your cassette player out to your garden, slap in your Sinatra tape, and talk to your little tomato plants or petunias as you tenderly place them in the ground. This is another inexpensive hobby with side benefits—flowers for the dinner table and tomatoes for the salad. Whenever you can, take all offers of free "slips" from other gardeners. Roses and geraniums are just two plants that slip very well. Join your local garden club, and you'll have plenty of buddies to share the joy!

Musical hobbies. How about taking up the guitar or banjo? Or organ lessons? Or piano? If you already have the instrument, your only expense will be instruction books and music. Ask for these when it comes birthday time, and you can pursue this hobby practically free. Sure, it takes hours of practice to improve. What a great use of your time!

Writing. How about taking up writing as a hobby? It might even progress from avocation to vocation, as it did with me. There are so many outlets for your writing talent—writing for newspapers or magazines, newsletters or greeting cards. Or, how about submitting a script for your favorite television soap opera? Or, write a

> *"I think happiness in . . . retirement is in direct relation to diversity of interest."*
> Walter Cronkite

children's book, romance novel, spy thriller or cookbook? Once you get started on this hobby, you'll be hooked immediately, because there are writing clubs to join, contests to enter, conferences to attend, and classes to take. If this sounds interesting to you, I recommend that you subscribe to *Writer's Digest* magazine, (800)333-0133, and purchase the writer's Bible: *Writer's Market*, which can be purchased at your local bookstore or ordered by calling (800)289-0963. The magazine will help you start writing, and the book will do the same, plus supply you with thousands of markets for the type of writing you decide to pursue. A writing hobby can become addictive but satisfying, as well. Good luck!

Little theatre. If you've always been a frustrated thespian, here's your chance! All theatre groups are longing and begging for "mature" actors and actresses. It's really difficult to take a young person and apply enough makeup to convert him or her to the character of a grandparent, for example.

If you don't really want to be in the spotlight, all theatre groups welcome stagehands, costume mistresses and publicity chairmen. What an exciting pursuit for you—go for it!

Collecting. Whether you collect baseball cards, books, stamps, antique bottles or butterflies, your retirement years afford you the hours it takes to carefully search out, research, and classify your "finds." There are also clubs you can join where you can share and exchange information.

We collect antique bottles, which is doubly fun because we get to go on "digs." We feel like archaeologists as we scrape and claw through the earth around old family dumps, under one-hundred-year-old houses, or in creek beds. We keep our antique bottle book with us when we dig so that we can look up our finds on the spot. It's a really exciting hobby and gets you outdoors as well.

By the way, some of the most valuable whiskey bottles are found buried under outhouses because in the olden days "Mama" wouldn't let "Papa" drink alcohol, so he would sneak to the outhouse, down his bottle, and drop it down the hole, never to be seen again. Pretty clever!

If you never had the time or patience to pursue a hobby, this is the perfect time to consider one. In fact, try out several things until you find one that suits you perfectly. Just be careful to consider the cost of your hobby; you're on a budget, remember? Luckily, most hobbies take more time than money.

Recreation

Senior center. Your local center is loaded with recreational ideas, from card playing to checkers to watching travelogues. Be sure to get on the mailing list so you can see what's coming up. There will be more things to do than you have the time, even though you're retired!

Attend "free stuff." There are a dozen things for you to enjoy every weekend in your area. How about the county fair or the recreational vehicle show at the fairgrounds or the local boys Little League finals? Then there's the zoo and Museum of Natural History and the Botanical Gar-dens. Are you getting the idea?

Watch your local newspaper for free entertainment. Once you get the hang of it, you'll wonder why you ever thought you had too much time on your hands!

Socializing. Unless you're retiring in your hometown, you'll need to make new friends. This can be difficult for many, but you need to do it anyway. If you've moved to an established retirement community, you'll find that friends come "built-in" with your new life-style. Otherwise, you'll need to reach out to other retirees you meet, whether at church, on your block, or at a club meeting. Entertaining doesn't need to be expensive either. You could have a couple over, for example, for a "movie night." Rent a classic movie video, make popcorn, and serve it in "movie theatre popcorn sacks," along with a drink in a paper cup. Another icebreaker is to invite another couple to go on a picnic with you or to the beach or on a hike. Almost anything you do for free can be just as much fun as expensive forms of entertainment, such as inviting someone over for a fancy prime rib dinner! Forget the fancy stuff—other retirees on tight budgets appreciate the simplicity of pure friendships and will be relieved they don't need to "pay you back" with an expensive dinner of "equal value." Keep it simple—the best things in life truly are free!

Dating. For single retirees, there's a lot of fun out there for you as well. The same inexpensive ideas we've already discussed can serve as a date. Whether it's square dancing, going to the zoo, or cross-country skiing together, the date can be just as much fun as an evening at an expensive concert. Whether you're a man or a woman, take advantage of all the free group activities offered through your retirement community, if you live in one, or through your local senior center. These activities are great opportunities to meet someone who'll be a fun companion, and when you actually start to date, remember that free can be just as much fun as expensive. It's the quality of time spent together that counts.

Learning

Traditional. You may decide that now is a wonderful time for you to go back to college. Whether you're going for a degree from a junior college, university or graduate school, there's no reason why you can't study, learn, and reach your educational goals. Lots of retirees are doing it. In fact, one who works as a teacher with my husband retired from the Air Force a couple years ago, went back to college, received his teaching credential, and is now, at age fifty-five, teaching fourth grade. His college experience was a bridge between careers and now he's looking forward to retiring again some day. You may decide after returning to school that you haven't reached all your goals as yet, and who knows what new career may still lie ahead for you?

Other seniors enjoy pursuing formal education after retirement because for the first time in their lives they have the time to really absorb and enjoy the subject matter.

By the way, it may comfort you to know that a recent study done by Harvard University showed that older citizens can be as mentally sharp as those in the under-thirty-five group. The study showed that people can stay young mentally even when age robs them of physical health.

Non-traditional. Non-traditional learning includes classes taken through Continuing Education, Community Services and self-learning. There are so many exciting classes being offered these days from Beginning Writing to Computer Programming to Flower Arranging. You can pick and choose what interests you.

You can also receive informal instruction over your own TV set. Most of the public stations offer many interesting classes from cooking to learning a foreign language. Also, stations like the Discovery Channel have educational programs on nature and travel.

Reading. Here's an activity enjoyed by almost every retiree I interviewed. Those I spoke with said they spend hours at their local libraries, poking around, enjoying the newspapers and magazines as well as books they check out to take home. If you haven't really taken time to browse around a library lately, you'll be surprised to find the large selection of books on cassette, videos that can be checked out at no charge, and large-print books available for those of us who find ourselves squinting occasionally, even though we wear glasses.

Be wild and crazy—delve into different types of fiction and nonfiction than you've ever read before. You'll find there's a whole new world of information out there to absorb and enjoy now that you have the time.

Helping

Church or charity work. There's a great need for helpers in churches and charities, particularly at certain times of the year. At Thanksgiving, for example, volunteers are needed to cook for those who would have to go without. At Christmas you're needed to help distribute food and clothing to needy families. Of course, volunteers are also needed year-round to do bookkeeping, run the computer, stuff envelopes, make telephone calls, etc. Don't forget that your corporate business expertise or any skill you have from your workaday life can be put to good use. Nonprofit organizations cannot afford to hire someone to administrate a complicated program or train staff on using a new Macintosh computer, so they really appreciate your knowledge and ability to help their organization work more effectively.

There's actually an organization called the Service Corps for Retired Executives (SCORE) that donates its time to helping troubled nonprofit organizations with their budgetary or managerial problems. Here are some services these retirees offer for free:

• *Long-range planning*
• *Marketing*
• *Personnel management*
• *Facilities planning and construction*
• *Budget, finance and resource allocation*
• *Public relations and publications*
• *Office practices and allocations*

You retired executives have valuable skills that are needed out there in the "world of volunteerism." There are too many opportunities out there for you to feel useless and unfulfilled after retirement.

Likewise, whatever your skill may be, whether you're a plumber, teacher or truck mechanic, you can become an appreciated volunteer.

One couple I know became involved with the "Make-a-Wish Foundation." They helped raise money to send a terminally ill child to Disneyland. They said the joy of that experience was more fulfilling than anything they had ever done before retirement. And their only expense was their time. You could never convince this couple that the retirement years aren't the best years of your life! You can contact "Make a Wish" at: Make a Wish Foundation of America, 2600 N. Central Ave., Suite 936, Phoenix, AZ 85004; (602)240-6600.

"Youth and seniors together." This is a program where a senior is matched up with a homeless kid who needs all kinds of help: a tutor, surrogate parent, role model, or just a good buddy and friend. Take the kids to the library or a ball game or to get an ice cream at Baskin-Robbins. In many cities this program is sponsored by the Salvation Army. Give them a call. You'll really feel you're needed and appreciated when you help out in this way.

Nursing home or hospital helper. We all know about the "Pink Ladies" or the "Candy-Stripers" who work at the local

---

A center for human services that provides peer support groups and workshops for women in transition, needs telephone answering volunteers.
This was a recent ad on the "Lend A Hand" page of a Modesto, California newspaper.

---

hospital, and you can become one of these needed volunteers. You can work for any number of hours or days a week that suits your schedule and, as an added bonus, you'll form friendships with the other workers that can last the rest of your life.

It takes a special person to work with those in nursing homes, those who have had strokes or can't communicate for some other reason. Here's an outlet for your love and care. Believe me, the staff of these hospitals will do handstands when they see you coming in the door. You really help them out as well.

Help your local school-teacher. My husband teaches fourth grade and is an excellent example of school teachers who would appreciate your help. He teaches a bilingual class of Hispanic children who speak very little English. He could use three or four of you every day of the week to read to the children, help them spell out English words, or even to bring Valentine treats or Christmas surprises. My mother volunteers in this way and is appreciated by a kindergarten teacher in the town where she lives; Mom reads to the kids once a week. The teacher selects five children who deserve a special treat, and they snuggle around my mom, who reads them a story, complete with sound effects. The children really get into the stories and treat mom like their "grandma." She brings the children little gifts such as bookmarks to encour-

The National Council for the Homeless reports that an estimated 500,000 children across the United States do not have homes.

age reading. She has also worked at school libraries, helping with the selection and purchase of new books.

Another way to help out is to become a tutor; call your local superintendent's office to see if there's a program in your area. If not, contact the National Association of Partners in Education, 601 Wythe St., Suite 200, Alexandria, VA 22314; (703)836-4880. Or order *Becoming a School Partner, AARP Fulfillment EE083* (address in Appendix A).

Knowing school teachers as I do, I'm sure you could be kept busy five days a week for the rest of your life.

Political campaigner. Here's your chance to make a difference. Instead of complaining about the "awful" candidates in office, as we all do, you can actually get someone new elected by making telephone calls, distributing flyers, and organizing rallies. In the process, you'll make a lot of good friends and have fun at the same time.

Keep your eyes and ears open for other volunteer opportunities; there are literally hundreds of thousands. If you would like help matching your interests and skills with the proper organization, just write AARP and ask to join their "Volunteer Talent Bank."

As I researched for this book, I interviewed retirees and asked them what they do with their leisure time. I also asked them how much money they spend on their leisure time activities. Here are some of their responses:

• *A couple in Waverly, Ohio said that she likes to quilt, sew, knit, read, and listen to music and he does woodworking and carving. They both bowl and play golf. Her hobbies cost about $15 a month and his less than $10; the bowling costs $15 a month, and the golf is $200 a year for both of them.*

• *Paul and Lois Gilbert, also from Ohio, like to read and listen to music. Lois knits and sews. They limit their TV watching. Their hobbies cost very little each month.*

• *A retired couple in San Ramon, California volunteers at the local senior center. She also belongs to a women's club. Their total leisure expense runs about $25 a month.*

• *A couple in Tampa, Florida, likes to read, bowl, and play golf. They spend about $100 a month.*

• *One of the several couples I interviewed at Pine Lakes Country Club in North Fort Myers, Florida, likes to entertain, do woodworking and crafts. They spend about $50 a month.*

By the time you pursue a couple of hobbies, play a few sports, go to the library, practice the piano an hour a day, and put in ten hours at your volunteer job, there's no way you'll be one of those who says: "I'm bored; I have too much time on my hands."

I think journalist Bard Lindeman said it best: "Life after work is not for retirement; it's for learning, for exploring, for adventure and, above all, growing. You are among the first pioneers of leisure, but that leisure comes with running shoes, a workout suit and a contract that reads: 'Serve others. Now!'"

Chapter Ten

Follow the Yellow Brick Road

[Affordable Retirement Travel]

Oh, you lucky retirees! You not only have time to travel, you can afford it now by following the tips in this chapter.

According to statistics, about 30 percent of you are "stay-at-homers," but the rest of you are just dying to go somewhere. In fact, 70 percent of all retired Americans take at least one vacation each year. Here are dozens of ways to afford travel on a small budget.

Pay Less for Airfares

Discount senior fares. Most airlines offer discount rates to seniors who are at least sixty-two or sixty-five years of age. A list of those that do and their telephone numbers appear in Appendix A.

Maxi saver fares. Many times you can get an airfare even lower than your senior discounted fare by taking advantage of special rates open to all ages. Watch for discounted fares called "Super Savers" or "flexible fares," which means that your time is flexible and you're available to fly whenever the best rates exist, even if the flight stops at various cities along the way.

"Hidden city" airfare. Savvy travelers are catching on quickly to the fact that very often you can cut your airfare by hundreds of dollars by booking a one-way

ticket to a city *past your destination*, but getting off the airplane when it has a stopover at your destination.

Let me give you an actual example of a certain traveler's use of this "Hidden City" technique: He wanted to fly from Boston to Dallas, but the fare was $571 one way, so he booked a flight from Boston to New Orleans with a stopover in Dallas for $99, with a savings of $471. It just happened that there was a special rate from Boston to New Orleans that happened to have a stop in Dallas anyway.

There are two things you must do to make this idea work:

---

1. You must *carry your luggage onto the plane with you or it will end up at the final stop!*

2. You must *book a one-way ticket, although you'll have another one-way ticket in your other pocket that will get you from Dallas back to Boston, probably on a different "Hidden City" airfare.*

Book fares early. There are various savings you can receive by booking your flight fourteen to sixty days in advance.

Companion fares. Companion tickets are sometimes available for free up to

$50. These fares are offered from time to time as advertising gimmicks and come with a lot of restrictions, such as being non-refundable, require a Saturday night stay, must be paid for seven to fourteen days in advance, etc.

Shop for best buys. This sounds like awfully elementary advice, but many people don't know that air fares vary considerably from airline to airline. Call them all when you're pricing airfares; don't ask your travel agent to do this for you because they may not have the time and patience that you have to check out every possibility. Prices will vary according to stopovers, day of the week, time of day, by paying in advance, etc.

Get out a huge pad of paper and play detective. When you've found the best deal, go through your travel agent, if that is most convenient for you. Remember that when you fly on any given flight, the passengers aboard have probably paid a dozen different prices to take this same exact flight. You can be the one who gets the best deal by doing your homework! You have plenty of time for this pesky job, so you might as well make it pay off in dollars.

Yearly pass or coupon book. If you plan to fly a great deal in one year's time, you may want to consider purchasing a pass that will save you a lot of money on each flight. Call the numbers in Appendix A to ask about current rates.

Buy as part of package tour. Most airlines offer package tours with the air-

A policeman must read you your rights if you're arrested, but a travel agent is not required to read you the fine print on your airline ticket.

fare thrown in. Call the same numbers and ask about any package plans to your destination.

Fly standby. If your schedule is really flexible and you don't mind keeping your bags packed by the front door day and night, do I have a deal for you. You can receive greatly discounted airfares, as well as other travel fares by "standing by" to take last-minute unsold space. An organization called Mature Outlook (through Sears) has a program called "Travel Alert" that can help you fly standby. Write or call them at: Mature Outlook Travel Alert, 6001 N. Clark St., Chicago, IL 60660; (800)336-6330.

Other Forms of Transportation

Travel by Rail
Amtrak. If you're sixty-five or older you can receive a 25 percent discount on Amtrak, (800)872-7245.

Via Rail Canada. If you plan to travel by rail in Canada, you can buy a forty-five-day pass. The rates vary according to "High Season" or "Low Season." Call Via Rail Canada at (800)361-3663.

Order a copy of "Fly-Rights," a list of your legal rights as a flyer on commercial airlines, from U.S. Dept. of Transportation, 400 Seventh St., S.W., Washington, DC 20590.

Travel by Bus

Greyhound/Trailways. You can receive a 10 percent discount if you are sixty-five and older.

Voyageur Inc. and Voyageur Colonial. In Canada you can receive up to one-third off regular fares as a senior discount. There are restrictions that apply, however.

Gray Line Sight-seeing, Inc. If you show your AARP membership card when you purchase your ticket at a Gray Line terminal or on board, you will receive 15 percent off fares for half or full-day tours at participating locations in the U.S. and Canada. These are the only locations that do not participate: Phoenix; Eureka Springs, Arizona; Denver; Miami; Savannah, Georgia; Las Vegas; Albuquerque; Seattle; Jackson Hole, Wyoming.

Travel by Personal Car

Save money when traveling by car:

Pack picnic baskets to avoid restaurant expenses.

Don't overload a car-top carrier; the wind resistance will lower your gas mileage.

Purchase your gas at the self-service pumps.

Join a motor club before you take off on a trip to avoid expensive towing or repairs on the road. Your own car insurance company probably offers a motor club membership; if not, try one of the clubs listed in Appendix A.

Take advantage of all the free things to see and do wherever you go. Call for free tourist information from each state's Bureau of Travel and Tourism; the telephone numbers are listed in Appendix A in the back of this book, along with ad-

dresses for the departments of tourism for all the regions of Canada. I also recommend a book called *Free Attractions, U.S.A* by Mary Van Meer and Michael Anthony Pasquarelli, which is available at your local library. Another helpful book is called the *Allstate Motor Club National Park Guide*, published by Prentice-Hall Travel.

Travel by Rental Car

Many car rental agencies offer senior discounts. See Appendix A for a list. Don't forget what we said in Chapter Seven about the CDW insurance offered by car rental agencies. Save up to $17 a day by saying "No" to this insurance if you're already covered on your own auto policy.

Travel by RV or Travel Trailer

Those seniors who have RVs really love them and would travel no other way. They not only make for economical traveling, they provide cozy home comforts as well. How else can you have your very own bed and pillow every night, your clothes and dishes in place, and many comforts of a motel room at a fraction of the cost?

You not only save on lodging, but on food as well, because you can cook on board your RV and spend your leftover travel money on things you really want to do.

If you aren't sure about this type of travel, rent an RV before purchasing one. Most rental agencies offer senior discounts including one of the largest called Cruise America. They offer a 10 percent discount to AARP members. Contact them at (800)327-7778.

Their twenty-four-foot unit sleeps six and rents for about $60 a day. We rented one of these units and were impressed with the cleanliness and low mileage.

If you think you would like to join an RV caravaning club, you may be interested in the fully escorted motorhome tours offered by RV Adventure Caravan, % Sierra RV, P.O. Box 18070, Reno, Nevada 89511. If you become serious about this RVing way of life, you may want to join The Good Sam Club, which is an international organization of RVers. They offer travel tours all over the world, many of them "caraventures," regular outings and camp outs, plus discounts on fees and RV expenses. They also have a chapter called "The Wandering Single Sams" for all you folks who are legally single and have an RV or a tent. The best thing they offer, however, is emergency road service. Membership is $15 a year. Write them at the address in Appendix A.

Travel Via Planned Tours for Seniors

The National Tour Association is a nonprofit trade organization that offers tours from the Canadian Rockies to the Old South and from the California Coast to New England. Their many different tours come in various price ranges, but some are definitely geared to retirees who are on a small budget. To find their address and to see a complete listing of other seniors organizations that offer planned tours for their membership, see the Travel section in Appendix A.

> *For motion sickness, ask your doctor to prescribe Transderm Scope. One medicated patch behind your ear will protect you for seventy-two hours.*

Lodging

Hotels and motels. See the list in Appendix A of motels and hotels that offer discounts to seniors. These can range from 10 to 50 percent, depending on time of year and day of the week. Most of the discounts are available to those fifty years or older, especially if they can show an AARP card.

Camping. You can rent a campsite for your RV or tent from $1.50 to $30 a night. Some sites are private and some public, and they vary as to facilities offered. This is obviously a moneysaving idea. Sources of campsite information can be found in Appendix A.

Hostels. You thought hostels were just for college kids, right? Not anymore. You can get a membership in the American Youth Hostels and stay in them anywhere in the world at low costs. In case you're not familiar with hostels, they're inexpensive accommodations for travelers offering only the minimum requirements: a clean bed, shower and bathroom. Many hostels have dormitory-style rooms with beds lined up in a row, one room for the men and one for the women, plus one men's and one women's bathroom to be shared by all the guests. Most hostels, however, offer nicer facilities with private rooms, although small and humble, shared bathrooms, a minimal dining room, and a few services, such as movies in the evening, bicycle rentals, Ping-Pong tables, and even barbecue grills. It's a little bit like "going to camp." I've interviewed many travelers who have stayed at hostels, and I've heard mixed reviews. Some think they're wonderful and others are offended by the minimal standards. Everyone said that prices seem to vary arbitrarily, and not according to quality. The rates vary from around $10 a day. If hosteling sounds interesting to you, write to the addresses in Appendix A.

Campus housing. If you're traveling when school is not in session you may be able to rent a dorm room at a college or university for about $15 a night. Sometimes meals are included. For information and a free directory see Appendix A.

Bed and breakfasts. This fad has really caught on in the past ten years. You get a "bed and breakfast" as a package deal, and usually for less than by purchasing lodging and breakfast separately. They are appealing because you get the warm atmosphere of a personal home, including "home cooking." I recommend a book called *Bed and Breakfast North America* by Norma Buzan. It's also available at your local library.

Stay at a "Y." YMCA's all over the country still offer safe and comfortable accommodations at very low rates. Usually you'll have use of all their facilities as well, including the swimming pool and fitness room. Make your reservations at least two months early.

Stay at an auto-truck stop. Have you been to a truck stop lately? They've changed from years gone by; now they offer pleasant rooms at a third of regular motel rates. They also have lots of convenient services such as barber shops, laundromats, restaurants and shopping.

Truckers have first choice, so always call ahead to see if there is "space available." It's worth the try for the quality you'll get for the money!

Stay for free by trading houses. There are many organizations that coordinate the trading of homes or apartments, where you can stay in a choice of homes or apartments by agreeing to make your home avail able. This has to be the best idea yet for those of us on a budget. See Appendix A for organizations that offer this service.

Cruising

Cruising can give you a lot for your money because for one all-inclusive price, you get your hotel room, recreation, meals, transportation and entertainment. There's no need to rent a car, search out restaurants, make hotel reservations, or pay for separate plane flights to your destination. Many cruise lines even include airfare in their package price. For a total of $1,146 one Caribbean cruise line offers a one-week budget cruise that includes:

Package price, including airfare:	*$1,041*
Meals	*Included*
Entertainment	*Included*
Bar	*60*
Gratuities	*45*
Total:	*$1,146*

Luxury versions of the same thing will run higher, usually closer to $2,000. However, you can cut these prices as much as 50 percent, or more, by:

• *Booking an "inside" rather than an "outside" cabin.*
• *Booking your cruise during the*

"shoulder" or off-seasons.
• Booking your cruise and paying a deposit as much as one year ahead.
• Booking your cruise at the very last minute, taking advantage of their "unbooked space" bargains. Call the cruise company directly to make these arrangements.
• Asking for the cruise line's regular senior discount.
• Booking a freighter cruise. A freighter is one of the big ships that delivers oil or other commodities to foreign companies. This is a very reasonable way to go. Your total price will run about $100 a day per person, and you'll be treated like a "special guest" because you'll be one of only ten to twenty passengers. You'll usually dine with the captain and his crew at mealtimes, and you'll be able to go on shore to sightsee at every port where the freighter is making deliveries.

One retiree in Fort Myers, Florida, said she always books her cruises at the very last minute. This saves her half or more of the regular price, and it also gives her the chance to see how she is feeling and whether she's in the mood for a cruise when the time comes.

Adventure Travel

Just because you're retired doesn't mean you're ready to "sit, soak, and sour." Many of you are so glad to be rid of the trappings of life that you can't wait to do something adventurous—something a little thrilling and chilling for a change. Well, there's a whole world of adventure out there for you folks. The contact and other information for organizations and companies offering adventure travel tours can be found in Appendix A. Here are some ideas.

Be a cowboy-for-a-week. Ride the range; work up a few saddle sores; help with the roundup. This is for real! You'll help drive six hundred head of cattle eighty miles, starting about three hours outside Reno in Nevada's Black Rock Desert. Or you may work on Spanish Springs Ranch in California's Lassen County. Git along, little doggies!

Archaeologist vacations. Excavate beads of amethyst and jade from two-thousand-year-old sites or observe the Quetzal bird as it nests in the cloud forests of southern Mexico. The Foundation for Field Research is looking for volunteers to join professional researchers on expeditions all around the world. No experience is necessary, and your contribution to cover food, lodging and research expense is tax deductible.

Go exploring. Travel to an out-of-the-way corner of the world: the Falklands, the Galapagos, Antarctica, Easter Island, etc. The ports of call are the stuff dreams are made of. You'll actually team up with scholars aboard one of two vessels that sail year-round on all the seas in the world.

Scuba diving vacations. Why not take up scuba diving? If you've never tried it, you can take lessons very reasonably through adult education classes in your area. If you don't live near a lake or ocean, classes can be taught in a swimming pool.

Once you get the hang of it, you'll probably be hooked. After the initial expense of your gear, you can usually dive for free. If you really want to explore even deeper undersea worlds (up to 150 feet), you may want to get there via a submarine. Believe it or not, there are Canadian-built Atlantis subs of up to eighty tons that have carried over 140,000 passengers on explorations of reefs and wrecks off the Cayman Islands, Barbados and the U.S. Virgin Islands. Or they'll also take you to Guam and the Hawaiian Islands of Oahu and Hawaii.

White water rafting. If you've never been white water rafting, you're certainly in for the two necessary ingredients of adventure-travel: thrills and chills! You don't have to start by crashing between rocks or careening off a waterfall; you can start out nice and easy, and work up to the more dangerous and exciting stuff. Information is available by calling the headquarters for the national forests in each state.

Adventure biking. Five hundred miles on a bicycle — through hell or high water, come rain or shine. Just the opposite of the "couch-potato life-style." Right? Yes, you can ride five hundred miles in one week, or you can take any one of the other twenty-two biking treks organized each year by the American Lung Association. Their rides range from two days to nine days and from easy to strenuous.

Climb a mountain and more! Why? Because it's there, of course. If you're in excellent physical shape and want to go for the biggest thrills of all, you may want to contact some of the travel organizations that arrange this type of adventure

for those of us over fifty. In addition to mountain climbing, you can take "rough trekking" tours, strenuous backpack trips, or even ride an elephant while you explore a jungle.

Travel for Free

If you really want that cruise or tour, but you can't afford it at all, here are ways to have it anyway:

Arrange a group tour. By putting together a group of fifteen to thirty people who want to go to the same destination, you can earn free passage. Call any travel agent, tour operator or cruise line for procedures and information. My travel agent said that anyone who comes into her office and says, "I have ten couples who want to take a certain tour. May I have my passage for free if I book these ten couples with you?" she will gladly exchange free passage for your trouble.

Become a tour guide or manager. You don't need to be an expert to qualify, just be willing to learn and take charge. I have a friend, for example, who is a history professor at the local university. He gets free trips a couple times a year by agreeing to guide a tour through a certain part of the world. Call your travel agent for more detailed information.

Present a lecture or program. By speaking only a couple times on a cruise, you can earn free passage. If you have any area of expertise such as nutrition, cook-

Brigham Young University has a toll-free senior helpline. For a directory of messages call (800)328-7576.

ing, history or geography, or if you're an entertaining speaker such as a humorist, magician or puppeteer, you may be just what a cruise line is looking for. Here are three recent titles of cruise lines' programs:

• *"Secrets for Women in Their Prime"*
• *"Health and Beauty Secrets Movie Stars and Celebrities Learn From Their Doctors"*
• *"You Can Look and Feel Younger at Any Age"*

If you're interested in pursuing the possibility of presenting a program on a cruise, follow these procedures:

• *Call each cruise line and ask them to send guidelines for submitting your credentials.*
• *Write up some snappy topic titles that will be suitable to the passengers taking particular cruises.*
• *Give a brief description of each potential presentation. (Use two or three sentences for each.)*
• *Be prepared to send a photograph of yourself in addition to a videotape of a presentation. (The video can be self-made or recorded by a friend.) Always send a* copy *of the original videotape.*

The cruise lines say that the two things they look for are: *humor* and *being entertaining*. Get a list of cruise lines from your travel agent or the Cruise Line International Association.

If you're a single man and are willing to provide platonic friendship to single women on board a cruise, you can earn free passage for yourself. It will mean dan-

cing, participating in games, playing cards, etc. The official name of this position is a "Host." I called my travel agent today to ask her about this idea, and she said that the cruise lines have very high standards. They want "mature" men with excellent manners, and they do a thorough background check. As of the date this book went to press, the Royal Cruise Line seemed to be hiring the largest number of hosts, although my travel agent said that it will vary from time to time. You really need to write or call every cruise line if you are interested in applying. Write Cruise Line International Association for a list of cruise lines to contact. ***By working even part-time*** for a travel agency you will be able to take advantage of gratuity travel offered to the employees of the company. If you really love to travel and probably need a little extra spending money anyway, why not train to become a travel consultant?

Need a Travel Partner?

Many of you retirees are single or must travel alone because your spouse is unable to travel with you. Fortunately, there are others like you who are looking for travel partners.

The organizations that will pair you with a traveling companion or that have trips planned especially for single mature travelers can be found in Appendix A.

Discount Clubs

There are many discount clubs you can join by paying a yearly fee. As a member of these clubs, you'll be able to save about 50 percent off the regular prices of hotels, motels, meals, entertainment and even tourist attractions. Some of these clubs will issue a plastic card to be used at the establishments that honor the discount; other clubs issue discount coupon books. These clubs are listed in Appendix A.

So, you see? You have no excuses! I've given you dozens of ways to take retirement trips on a small budget—don't say you can't afford it! Have a great time and send me a postcard.

Chapter Eleven

How to Make Money Without Really Working

[Stretching Your Investment Income]

Now that you've discovered all the ways to cut down on your spending, you may still be coming up short. The answer to this dilemma, of course, is to generate more income, and this can be done several ways. One is to handle your liquid assets more wisely by investing your income to the maximum without jeopardizing the principal. Another way is to sell some of your nonliquid assets such as your family home. Other things you might consider would be to start a home business, work part-time, turn your hobby into income, or work seasonally as you feel up to it. We'll examine these options here and in Chapter Twelve.

The time when retirees need some extra money is usually not after they begin receiving Social Security benefits, but from the date of their early retirement until age fifty-nine and a half when their IRAs, pensions or Keoghs begin paying a monthly income. Let's say that due to the Golden Handshake, job burnout or poor health you retired at age fifty-four. Be-

> *Beware of anyone who says he can "make you rich" by selling you an investment.*

cause you retired so young, you probably don't have the nest egg you were expecting; however, you still have five and a half years before your retirement pensions kick in, and eight and a half years before you can begin receiving Social Security. So, these are the "crunch" years where you must either tighten your belt and reduce your expenditures considerably, or supplement your income by bringing in the extra.

Income From Liquidated Assets

As we mentioned in Chapter Two, if you or your spouse is at least fifty-five, you can take your onetime $125,000 capital gains exemption on the sale of your home. That means you don't have to pay capital gains income tax on the first $125,000 in *profit* on the sale of your home. If you paid $80,000 for your home, added $25,000 in improvements, and sold it for $190,000, you'll be exempt from the profit of

$85,000. Talk with your tax adviser to get the details, but it may be advantageous for you to liquidate your equity to provide income. You may also decide to liquidate other assets such as your fishing boat or second car.

Income From a Reverse Mortgage on Your Home

Does it break your heart to sell your family home? Do your children and grandchildren still enjoy the old homestead? Well, dry your tears, because there *is* another way. If you're at least sixty-two, you can apply for a "Reverse Equity Mortgage" where you may receive a monthly income of $200 to $2,000 from your home equity. You can stay in your home for the rest of your life, and you never have to pay the mortgage back in your lifetime. See Chapter Two for a detailed explanation of this wonderful option.

A recent study conducted by the Capital Holding Corporation, a Louisville, Kentucky, based life insurance company that offers these reverse mortgages, showed that 67 percent of those seniors who applied for this type mortgage were doing so to have more money to improve their life-styles with discretionary purchases and activities. Only 33 percent were planning to use the money for day-to-day living expenses or for unexpected bills such as medical costs.

The beauty of this type mortgage is that it provides monthly payments to seniors, based on their age and equity in the home, while guaranteeing them lifetime occupancy of their homes.

Income From Wise Investments

Robert Martel of the Merrill Lynch Investment Company says: "You'll be very lucky indeed if Social Security and your pension provide half your retirement income." This means that your nest egg, as small as it may be, must be managed wisely to provide your remaining needs.

This brings us to the obvious question: How do we know how to manage our nest egg wisely? Some retirees depend entirely on their own judgment, some on the advice of stockbrokers, some on the advice of private financial advisers, while others read investment advice columns in newspapers or investment newsletters. Some listen to advice from experts over the radio or from those who write books.

My own preference is to gather advice from every source possible, then weigh it carefully. I never fall for one "expert's" recommendation, but I balance it against other recommendations I read or hear about. I also like to pick the brains of wise investor friends who I can *trust*.

One such friend, retired for several years, was a banker for more than thirty years and invests his nest egg in three ways: CDs, real estate mortgages, and a Christian investment trust that yields 9.5 percent interest over a locked five-year period. Another friend, a professor of economics at California State University—Stanislaus, Turlock, California, believes in tax-free municipal bonds. He buys only those that provide income that is exempt from both California and federal taxes.

Though I'm not an investment expert,

I'm happy to pass on the advice of many experts in the investment field. It's up to you to weigh it carefully and decide upon your own investment strategy.

Remember how tired and stressed you felt before you retired? You didn't have time to do the calling, reading, and checking around to find the right investments for you. But now that you're free, you have plenty of time, and you can put it to good use by moving your precious dollars around to give you the best possible retirement income for the years to come. Read books on the subject, too. One of the best is called *Keys to Retirement Planning* by Warren Boroson, a Barron's Business Keys book. It's not only a very helpful book for anyone, but it's especially written for those of you who are entering retirement.

If you would really like to have a personal one-on-one guru who can help you sort through the hundreds of ways to invest your precious money, many say that a private financial adviser might be a good idea. The key, however, is to find one who is a "fee-based planner" (as opposed to a "commission-based planner") and has a "C.F.P." designation. The fact that the planner receives no commission from the advice he gives means that the advice may be more objective. And the C.F.P. title means that he has attended the College for Financial Planning and has received a Certified Financial Planner designation. See Appendix A for two associations that can recommend financial advisers with these qualifications.

Others recommend the advice of tried and true public financial advisers such as Jane Bryant Quinn, my personal favorite. In one of her recent columns she recommended do-it-yourself retirement planning kits such as the free one T. Rowe Price, which can be ordered by calling (800)458-9877. I ordered one of these kits for myself, and I'll pass some of their advice on to you.

T. Rowe Price suggests three portfolios: I (Low Risk), II (Moderate Risk), and III (High Risk). They recommend Portfolio I for "those with a low tolerance for risk or who are nearing retirement. This approach emphasizes safety of principal through such investments as Treasury bills, money market funds or certificates of deposit. Growth is not abandoned, but the primary goal is protecting assets."

They say that Portfolio II is for someone near retirement "who can *assume more risk*, perhaps because he or she has other assets or sources of income." This portfolio emphasizes growth-oriented investments such as common stocks.

The highest risk, Portfolio III, is for the investor willing to assume "greater risk for potentially greater return, which designates 85 percent of the assets to growth." Although Portfolio III produces the best performance, it also experiences the highest volatility with its best year

> *If you invest $10,000 at 7 percent interest and withdraw $116 a month, how many years before the money is gone? Answer: Ten years.*

showing a 33.3 percent profit and its worst year a loss of 22.6 percent. This type portfolio is recommended only for those who have a long time before retirement. (Their Portfolio I, on the other hand, provided the "lowest annualized return over the past two decades, but it also had the lowest volatility and did not suffer a loss in any single year.")

Everyone knows that the higher the risk you take in investing, the greater your potential return, but high risk investing takes a great deal of emotional fortitude to live with its volatility. There is, as one expert describes it, the "sleep factor," which means that you shouldn't invest in anything that will cause you to lie in bed at night losing sleep over it. If you can sleep like a puppy with a tummy full of milk, go for it.

Speaking of the "sleep factor," be sure to place your money with a savings institution that is federally insured either by the FDIC (banks) or the FSLIC (savings and loans). Also, limit each account to the $100,000 maximum guaranteed by these agencies.

Most experts advise that you're losing money unnecessarily by keeping it in a "passbook savings account" or checking account at only 5.25 percent or so. You could place your money in a money market deposit account that may yield between 7 and 10 percent, while having the same accessibility to your money. This is a fairly new thing, and if you haven't heard about it yet, ask your lending institution. Your money will be safe and accessible while earning a higher rate of interest.

In general, all financial experts agree that investments fall into four categories: Very High Risk, High Risk, Moderate Risk

and Minimum Risk. In the book *Retiring Right* by Lawrence J. Kaplan, he breaks down these risk categories into these types of investments:

Very high risk. (Can be called gambling.) Commodities futures, options, collectibles, oil and gas ventures, raw land, precious metals, penny stocks, foreign stocks and margin accounts.

High risk. (Some elements of speculation.) Common stocks of low quality, new issues of stocks and bonds, speculative grade bonds with the following ratings — Standard & Poor's: BB, B, CCC, CC, D; Moody's: Ba, B, Caa, Ca, C.

Moderate risk. (Regular income and potential long-term growth.) Blue Chip stocks and preferred stocks, investment grade corporate and municipal bonds with these ratings — Standard & Poor's: AAA, AA, A, BBB; Moody's: Aaa, Aa, A, Baa. Variable annuities, investments and real estate other than your own home, stock and bond mutual funds whose goals are income and long-term growth.

Minimum risk. (Safe, liquid, good yield.) Bank money market accounts, money market mutual funds, insured CDs, U.S. Treasury paper (bills and notes), tax-exempt bond mutual funds, individual tax-exempt municipal bonds rated AAA.

If you should decide to include mutual funds in your portfolio, most agree you should always buy those with "No-load," which means you won't have to pay a fee to purchase or sell your mutual funds. For a list of the mutual funds that do not levy any sales charges or commissions, see Appendix A.

I notice that real estate investments (other than your own home) fall under the moderate risk category, but I found that many retirees I interviewed are doing very well with these investments. The key is to know what you're doing; if you don't, stay out of it.

One popular idea is to purchase a vacation home to rent out most of the year. This can provide you growth in equity, a free vacation, added income, and a tax shelter. Mortgage interest and property taxes for a second or vacation home may qualify as itemized deductions on Schedule A of your income tax returns, right along with your principal residence deductions. If you don't rent this second home for any part of the year, your only income tax deductions for it are the mortgage interest and property taxes. However, if you rent it out for part of the year, additional expenses may also become tax deductions. Check with your tax adviser on all the details. But regardless of the tax ramifications, your money will be invested in something that may be appreciating and making you money overall.

Another way retirees use real estate as a moneymaking venture is to buy run-down homes, fix them up, and resell them for a profit. Obviously, you'll need to know your market value well enough to buy low, put minimum cash into it, and resell at a profit. This is tricky, but can be done. This is an especially good idea for the retiree who is handy and can work fast.

I know one retired couple who works as a team. He does the heavy stuff—carpentry, cement work, roofing, etc. She does the lighter work, such as painting, wallpapering and landscaping. They take a home, work on it for eight weeks, and turn it over for about $15,000 in profit.

They only "work" on one home each year to help them stretch their income.

Investing in raw land, you'll notice, falls into the very high risk category, although people I know personally are doing very well in this form of speculative investing. Most of those I interviewed were buying lots in the first filings of subdivisions, then reselling in a year or two when the prices had risen with each new filing. A "filing" contains a certain number of parcels of land, or lots, and is recorded in the county records. A new subdivision may, for example, have a total of five "filings." The sale of subdivision lots usually starts with "Filing No. 1." When all those lots are sold out, the next filing is opened up for sale. Each new filing that goes up for sale will probably have lots with higher prices than the previous filing, so many investors make money by merely purchasing in the first filing and selling when the last filing goes on the market, thus taking advantage of the subdivider's pricing strategy.

Beware of Scams

This is probably a good time to talk about the scam artists out there, waiting to prey on the poor retiree who is desperately wanting to generate income from his available cash. The con men know you're eager and vulnerable, so watch out!

Here are some unfortunate examples of victims who "got took":

• *A retired Wantagh, New York, engineer named James Hughes, age sixty-seven, invested $14,000 (over the objections of his wife, Dorothy) in Gold Coast Rarities. Gold Coast claimed to be marketing "rare, uncirculated coins" and prom-*

ised to repurchase its coins after a year at a guaranteed profit of 15 percent. He never received any coins at all and other investors who did discovered they weren't rare. The company has since gone bankrupt and the owner was convicted of fraud.

• *Paul Collins, age seventy-one, former superintendent of a California public school system, lost $225,000 by investing with the Precious Metals Accumulation Corp. of Newport Beach, California. He saw the ad on television.*

• *Victoria Hightower lost $10,000 in 3,500 shares of a gold-mining firm and 4,500 shares of a venture-capital company. A year after purchasing these shares she found that the gold company had merely owned land near a mine.*

• *Greg Capps purchased fifteen "Salvador Dali" prints for $12,700 from two telemarketers. They turned out to be worthless.*

Telemarketers are those people who call you during dinner and ask a question like: "If you could make 30 percent on your savings in the next three months without taking any risks, would you be interested?" Only an idiot wouldn't want such a deal, right? So, many people tend to keep listening. What they don't realize is that the telemarketer on the other end is highly trained, with a script, and he knows exactly what to say to get you to agree.

The reason you're called in the first place, by the way, is often because you have been put on lists that are sold to con artists by credit card companies or others who have sold you something over the telephone before. Believe me, whenever you purchase something over the telephone, your name and number go on lists that are sold for profit all over the nation, lists that are purchased by all degrees of scum and sleaze. It isn't by mere chance that you're called.

These are three good rules to follow:

• *Never purchase anything over the telephone.*
• *Never give your credit card number to anyone who calls you on the telephone.*
• *If it sounds too good to be true, IT IS!*

There is also a soft-sell kind of scam that goes on all the time in the investment business. It is called: **"Don't let the customer read the fine print."** You see, many legitimate-sounding investments have loopholes. For example, one ad suggested getting out of CDs and into U.S. government notes and bonds. The ad said the security couldn't be better because the United States guarantees all of your money. What the *fine* print says, however, is that the value of your principal will fluctuate with the up and down swing of interest rates.

Many annuities that are advertised as having an extra large interest rate of 13 percent that is "safe and guaranteed" are really only an 8 percent annuity with a 5 percent bonus for the first year. If you try to get out of the annuity early, you not only lose most of the 5 percent bonus, but you have a surrender charge on the amount of money you invested.

Another potential gimmick is a mutual fund that is invested in U.S. bonds or notes with a high "payout," such as 11 percent. While these funds do have a "payout" of 11 percent, they aren't earning that much "interest," but are slowly returning your own principal to you. Do you see how they trick people? They use the word "payout" to make you believe you're getting a lot in "interest," but they're actually paying a low interest rate and only returning your principal to make up the difference. What a shock!

Check, double-check, and read the fine print! You'll find that a little common sense and "Caveat Emptor" will let you join the ranks of retirees who are using their assets to generate the highest possible monthly income.

Chapter Twelve

Keep a Little Jingle in Your Jeans

[Rewarding Ways to Make Ends Meet]

Your assets are one valuable resource of income; a second resource is found in your own abilities, training, experience and creativity. There are ways to use this second resource to make ends meet, without the stress you felt before retirement.

One thing you should know up front is this: If you suffered burnout on your pre-retirement job, you should definitely avoid that same type work now. This is the time in your life when you need something fun and invigorating—something new and challenging that will bring in those extra needed retirement dollars.

If you're already receiving Social Security benefits, be aware that you're limited in the amount of money you can earn each year without losing some of these benefits. As of 1991 the annual limit is $9,720 for people sixty-five through sixty-nine, and $7,080 for those under sixty-five. There's no limit for people age seventy and older. If you exceed the limit, some of your benefits will be withheld.

> *"He is well paid that is well satisfied."*
> Shakespeare

You will lose $1 for every $2 of benefits if you're under sixty-five, and $1 for every $3 of benefits if age sixty-five through sixty-nine.

Income From a Home Business

There are hundreds of ways you can make money in your very own home. In a new book titled *The 100 Best Spare-Time Business Opportunities Today*, Kevin Harrington and Mark Cohen say, "There are plenty of part-time business opportunities that not only provide extra money, but easily fit into your life-style." They say the first steps in choosing the right spare-time business for you are to ask: Can I afford it? Do I like it? Will it be easy to learn? Will it be easy to run? Does your city or county allow you to run a business out of your home?

Here are just a few of the thousands of ideas to whet your appetite:

• *Buy a franchise for a needed service,*

such as blind cleaning. You go to homes, remove their blinds, bring them to your garage, clean them, and re-hang them in the customers' home. Many service franchises such as these are available.
• *Become the middleman for a product such as Amway or Mary Kay cosmetics.*
• *Start a secretarial service in your home.*
• *Operate a telephone answering service out of your home.*
• *Offer a "wake-up" service for sleepy heads who must be up by a certain time.*
• *Open a dance or aerobics studio in your garage.*
• *Teach piano.*
• *Start a pet-sitting or house-sitting business. (I know from personal experience that you'll have all the business you can handle if you can babysit people's pets in your own home or yard.)*
• *Start a mail-order business.*
• *Start a catering business.*
• *Make custom T-shirts and caps to sell to sports teams or by mail-order.*
• *Buy anything wholesale and sell it retail out of your home or through direct mail.*
• *Start a pickup and delivery service for local businesses.*
• *Start a bed and breakfast; turn spare bedrooms into moneymaking travelers' havens.*
• *Turn your garage into a repair shop for sick clocks, bicycles, golf clubs, etc.*
• *Offer a desktop publishing service.*
• *Start a "headhunting" business (matching up employers with job-hunting potential employees)*
• *Start a home business for small businesses that can't afford a full-time professional consultant: accountants, book-keepers, lawyers, financial planners . . . you get the idea.*
• *Start a sharpening business in your garage (for tools, saws, scissors, etc.)*

As you can imagine, the list of possibilities would fill several fat volumes.

If you want to start a home business, you need to consider startup expenses you will have in each of the following categories: equipment (supplies, furniture, machines, etc.), licenses and fees, insurance, deposits, working capital and other miscellaneous expenses.

If you become serious about starting up a home-based business, don't try to "wing it." There are right and wrong ways of going about it, and you definitely need to get a copy of a book called *Entrepreneur Magazine's Complete Guide to Owning a Home-Based Business*. It will tell you how to "Gear Up," "Set Up Shop," "Run Your Business," "Live With Your Business," and handle growth and expansion. This helpful book also has a list of home-based franchises, including Video 5000, Yard Cards, Inc., The Screen Machine, Lube On Wheels, Haunted Hayrides, Critter Care, Bundle of Convenience, Intl., and The Weed Man. You may also want to subscribe to *Entrepreneur Magazine* so you can stay up to date and encouraged as you pursue your new venture.

You should also read the "Investment Opportunities" section of *U.S.A. Today* newspaper for franchise and business opportunities, and you'll want to take advantage of the publications and videotapes supplied by the U.S. Small Business Administration (address in Appendix A); these help anyone start and manage a successful small business out of his home.

Other associations and publications that will be helpful to you if you decide to start a home business are listed in Appendix B.

By the way, a fringe benefit of a home business is the tax advantage. Be sure to ask your tax adviser about the details.

Turn Your Hobby Into Income

While we're talking about a home business, why not turn your hobby into a little business? When you were working you were constantly frustrated because you didn't have enough time to work on your hobby, right? Well, here's the answer! Take your interest and expertise and turn them into extra income. Here are just a few ideas:

- *Quilt-making.*
- *Become a professional seamstress.*
- *Become an antique dealer and refinisher.*
- *Become a professional writer.*
- *Start a photography business; convert a bedroom or garage into a small studio.*
- *Woodworking (make birdhouses, Christmas tree decorations, old-fashioned children's toys, customized cases, etc.)*
- *Make and sell jewelry, belts, ceramics, etc.*
- *Paint (watercolors, acrylics, oils, tole)*
- *Make Christmas crafts, sell seasonally.*
- *Make cross-stitch or needlepoint accessories.*
- *Try songwriting.*
- *Invent something and sell the patent to*

a company.
- *Gift baskets.*
- *Garage sales. (Pick up bargains at others' garage sales or at flea markets, then turn these items over for a profit at your own continuing sales.)*
- *Teach workshops in your craft or expertise.*

Your crafts can be sold through many different sources, including mail-order, gift parties, by consignment at local shops, renting booths at local craft fairs, or through your own garage sales.

The garage sale idea is a good one because you can have these sales at your own convenience and when you've accumulated enough "trash and treasures" to make it worthwhile. For excellent advice, order *The Garage Sale Handbook* by Peggy Hitchcock, from Pilot Books, (516)422-2225.

Work Part-Time Outside the Home

For those of you who don't want to be bothered with a home business, or may not be the entrepreneurial type, perhaps you only want an interesting part-time job. However, remember what I said earlier about choosing something different and refreshing from your pre-retirement work, unless you really loved what you did before.

How about these possibilities?

- *Little League umpire.*
- *Receptionist at a doctor's office.*
- *Salesperson in a gift shop.*
- *Teacher's aide.*

• Take on a paper route.
• Help rock babies at a child care center.
• Fast food worker.
• School bus driver.
• Sales clerk.
• Nurse or nurses' aide.
• Librarian's assistant.
• Custodial assistant.
• School cafeteria worker.
• Hotel worker.

The list of part-time jobs is endless, of course; the important considerations are that the job sounds interesting to you and is within your physical abilities. Organizations that help seniors find part-time employment are listed in Appendix A.

You should also visit personnel departments and employment agencies, and read classified help wanted ads. You will need a current resume, which is a summary of your work experience, education and training. Your resume should include the following:

• Name, address and telephone number
• Job objective
• Work history
• Education and/or special training
• References

If you use the services of an employment agency, they will help you structure your resume, but be sure to apply for the positions that are "fee-paid." The employment fee is paid by the employer, not the employee.

When you go for your interview, dress nicely, slightly better than necessary. And if you send a thank you note after the interview, it's an extra plus for you. This is expected by today's standards, even if the position is part-time or temporary.

Income From Seasonal Work

Many seniors like the idea of seasonal or temporary work where they can do something for only a few months at a time. Some would rather take a temporary job full time than a steady job part time. That way they can look forward to a break where they have nothing but the leisure they expected upon retirement.

Temporary or seasonal work is the easiest to get because it doesn't work into the plans of most people. Here are a few of these opportunities:

• Work in a cannery.
• Work at a concession at a summer fair.
• Work in the home of a new mother until she gets back on her feet.
• Help out in the home of anyone who needs help when convalescing from an operation or serious illness.
• Teach summer school or work as an aide.
• Work in a summer recreation program, as a coach, lifeguard, instructor or office worker.
• Work for the U.S. Census Bureau as they need temporary workers.
• Train as an H&R Block employee so you can help people with their tax forms once a year. The IRS also uses seasonal help.
• Work as Santa or the Easter Bunny.
• Work as a guard at a construction site until job is completed.
• Hire yourself out "on contract" as needed, as an electrician, plumber, cab-

inet maker, cook, etc.
• *Help with golf course maintenance during the busy summer or winter months, depending on your part of the country.*
• *Work in a ski equipment rental shop during ski season.*
• *Work in a plant nursery in the spring or summer.*

Watch the classified ads for ideas and contact the temporary employment agencies in your area. Especially contact those schools, agencies, state fairs, food processors, etc. who normally hire on a seasonal or temporary basis. Get your application in, along with a professional-looking resume, and you'll find that this type work will be the easiest to get.

Don't be afraid to attend a trade school or specialty school for a few months to get into the type work you would enjoy. A very good example of this is a semi-retired woman I met in North Fort Myers, Florida, who needs to work until she begins collecting her Social Security benefits; however, she wants to delay taking her Social Security as long as possible so her benefit checks will be large enough to support her when she eventually retires completely. She is presently finishing up six months of training to learn massage so that she can work for a chiropractor as a contract masseuse. She'll need to pass a state test to become licensed, but she'll be achieving her goal of learning a more challenging and interesting occupation to provide income for the rest of her working life.

At Pine Lakes Country Club and Resort, a retirement community in North Fort Myers, Florida, many of the residents work part time for the community. The men like the paid duty at the guard gates where they not only pick up the "extra jingle" they need to make ends meet, but have a personal interest in keeping their community safe.

Sun City Tucson, a large retirement community, also hires many of its own residents as part-time help, and the workers love it. One lady I met served as a tour guide of the facilities, which gave her a chance to show off her community while getting paid.

Many of the "crafty" residents of Sun City Tucson work in their own gift shop where they sell the treasures they have made in the lapidary studio, wood shop, jewelry and pottery workshops. These folks are the perfect examples of turning hobbies into income. Their gift shop is provided by Sun City Tucson, and you should see it — it could've been transported right off Fifth Avenue in New York City! Their work is exquisite, and the prices are reasonable, yet it brings in the extra income needed for these retirees.

Don't forget that when you retire you still have about a third of your life left to live, so if you need to supplement your income, try out something that will thrill you — something creative and interesting. Whether you learn a new trade, start a business in your home, turn your hobby into income or just use your time more wisely by studying the art of investing your money, these are painless ways to add to your income. You'll be having so much fun you'll be the envy of all your buddies still trapped in their regular jobs. In fact, you'll be the inspiration for them to take the plunge into retirement, too.

Go for it! I'm cheering for you!

Chapter Thirteen

Time for the Bottom Line

[Affordable Retirement Budgets]

"A great retirement on a small budget"— is it really possible? It sure is, and the proof is in this chapter. In the process of researching this book I interviewed retirees all over the country. I wanted to know how much they spend on everything and how they prioritize their spending. Most interesting, however, are the ways they stretch their dollars.

Some retirees spend more on travel and Christmas than others. Some give 10 percent to their church; some don't. One of the most important factors was whether they have a house payment or not. For those who own their retirement abodes, there was obviously money left for the fun stuff—recreation, travel, eating out. There was also a huge variation in the cost of health insurance and care. Some of those I interviewed were very fortunate to have most of their health expenses paid by former employers as part of their retirement package.

Here are the actual budgets of some of the retirees I interviewed. You'll feel encouraged when you see how well these retirees are doing on their small budgets. You'll be able to compare your potential budget with theirs to see how you will do. On a national average, by the way, this is where retirees get their income:

Investments	*34%*
Employment	*24%*
Social Security	*21%*
Pensions	*19%*
Other	*2%*

The sources of income vary for those I interviewed.

Retired Singles' Budgets

Retired Single No. 1
Monthly Budget: $578

Sources of Income:

Social Security	*53%*
Pension	*27%*
Investments	*20%*

Monthly Spending:

Housing	*$225.00*
Utilities	*125.38*
Food	*100.00*
Eating Out	*16.00*
Church/Charities	*27.50*
Goods/Services	*14.50*
Insurance	*0*
Health Care	*6.60*

Transportation	20.00	Goods/Services	25.00
Leisure/Recreation/Hobbies	0	Insurance	185.00
Travel/Vacations	36.00	Health Care	0
Repairs	7.50	Transportation	70.00
Christmas giving	"Very Little"	Leisure/Recreation/Hobbies	30.00
		Travel/Vacations	100.00
		Repairs	41.67
		Christmas giving	12.50

Before I began the research on this book, I would have sworn that no one could live on so little, but this widow lives in Bristol Village, a retirement community in Waverly, Ohio, and seems really happy on her meager income. She says she is "extremely busy with many activities, international relations club, Enrichment Hour every Thursday, Vespers every Sunday evening, Saturday night potluck suppers, watercolor painting, sewing and knitting."

She states, "I do not spend much money. I enjoy magazines. I have sewed many of my clothes. I don't need to buy *any*!"

Her health insurance and medical costs are covered very well through the state of Illinois, for whom her husband worked for many years. She says for entertainment and recreation, she likes to walk and picnic at nearby Scioto State Park.

We should all be so easily satisfied!

This man owns a small home in the expensive San Francisco-Oakland Bay area of California. He likes to travel by car; he says tours are too expensive. He loves "scenic areas such as the California and Oregon coasts." He also visits museums. His health costs are covered by his insurance, but he tries to "stay clear of people with colds and flu." He enjoys the activities at the local senior center such as playing cards, and he shops only at thrift shops or when things are on sale. His food costs are so low because he's given surplus fruit by neighbors, and he eats a lot of beans and legumes. He says he buys only inexpensive breads such as plain whole wheat. He cooks four meals at a time, eats two and freezes two.

I'm familiar with the high cost of living in his area and, believe me, he is doing *very well*.

Retired Single No. 2
Monthly Budget: $840

Sources of Income:

Social Security	87%
Investments	13%

Monthly Spending:

Housing (taxes only)	$40.00
Utilities	140.00
Food	60.00
Eating Out	35.00
Church/Charities	100.00

Retired Single No. 3
Monthly Budget: $897

Sources of Income:

Social Security	75%
Pension	25%

Monthly Spending:

Housing	$150.00
Utilities	150.00
Food	150.00
Eating Out	20.00

Church/Charities	0
Goods/Services	52.00
Insurance	180.00
Health Care	50.00
Transportation	50.00
Leisure/Recreation/Hobbies	20.00
Travel/Vacations	42.00
Repairs	17.00
Christmas giving	16.00

This lady lives in California and retired at sixty-two for medical reasons. She likes her local senior center where she answers phones and takes writing and quilting classes. She buys clothing and dishes at thrift shops, and says she eats very well by "getting a lot of food donated by grocery stores through the senior citizens center." She spends about $500 a year on travel and enjoys block parties on holidays. She says that she was only "conned" into buying something once; she bought $29 worth of light bulbs that were so dim she couldn't use them.

Her statement that "my needs are few and simple" is certainly believable!

Retired Single No. 4
Monthly Budget: $923

Sources of Income:

Social Security	30%
Pension	55%
Investments	15%

Monthly Spending:

Housing	$300.00
Utilities	50.00
Food	150.00
Eating Out	100.00
Church/Charities	25.00
Goods/Services	50.00
Insurance	60.00

Health Care	39.00
Transportation	50.00
Leisure/Recreation/Hobbies	50.00
Travel/Vacations	0
Repairs	8.00
Christmas giving	41.00

This beautiful lady says that "since I retired, I don't buy much clothing, then only when it's on sale." She cuts down on food costs by watching for sales and using coupons. She retired from the state of California at sixty-seven and works as a volunteer Ombudsman.

Retired Single No. 5
Monthly Budget: $1,310

Sources of Income:

Social Security	32%
Pension	20%
Investments	48%

Monthly Spending:

Housing	$371.00
Utilities	110.00
Food	150.00
Eating Out	20.00
Church/Charities	209.00
Goods/Services	50.00
Insurance	31.17
Health Care	12.50
Transportation	15.00
Leisure/Recreation/Hobbies	0
Travel/Vacations	33.34
Repairs	8.34
Christmas giving	300.00

This retired lady, obviously, loves to give generously at Christmas, for at $300 a month toward gifts, she has a total Christmas budget of $3,600 a year. She explained that she has a large family, including six grandchildren. She lives in the Midwest and her travel includes two trips a year to visit her family. Her church activities are very important to her and she says: "I have *always* lived simply."

Retired Couples' Budgets

Retired Couple No. 1
Monthly Budget: $1022

Sources of Income:

Social Security	83%
Pension	14%
Investments	3%

Monthly Spending:

Housing (taxes only)	45.00
Utilities	$150.00
Food	300.00
Eating Out	100.00
Church/Charities	10.00
Goods/Services	50.00
Insurance	250.00
Health Care	0
Transportation	100.00
Leisure/Recreation/Hobbies	0
Travel/Vacations	0
Repairs	0
Christmas giving	16.67

This retired couple occupies themselves with volunteer work. They love to travel, but feel they can't afford it. They buy wash and wear clothes to save on dry-cleaning bills and also shop at thrift shops. They take the bus or walk whenever they can. They live in an expensive area of California but manage miraculously well on such a small budget.

Retired Couple No. 2
Monthly Budget: $1,127

Sources of Income:

Social Security	47%
Pension	48%
Investments	4%
Other	1%

(Sells crafts at annual craft fair)

Monthly Spending:

Housing	$352.00
Utilities	83.50
Food	250.00
Eating Out	30.00
Church/Charities	50.00
Goods/Services	145.00
Insurance	42.50
Health Care	20.00
Transportation	20.00
Leisure/Recreation/Hobbies	50.00
Travel/Vacations	30.00
Repairs	4.17
Christmas giving	50.00

This couple call themselves "stay-at-homes," but they do have hobbies. She's involved in three musical groups and likes to sew. By the way, she cuts her husband's hair, and they also save money by purchasing all their food through a warehouse food club.

They purchase generic drugs when possible, and travel "mostly to our children's homes." Once a year they go to a nearby state park on a three-day trip. She quilts, and he does woodworking and carving. They both bowl and play golf. He was sixty-two and she was sixty-three when they retired. They're glad they didn't wait any longer to retire because they are really enjoying it.

Retired Couple No. 3
Monthly Budget: $1,317

Sources of Income:

Social Security	56%
Pension	37%
Investments	7%

Monthly Spending:

Housing	$275.00
Utilities	75.00
Food	300.00
Eating Out	50.00
Church/Charities	50.00
Goods/Services	30.00
Insurance	185.00
Health Care	150.00
Transportation	60.00
Leisure/Recreation/Hobbies	30.00
Travel/Vacations	100.00
Repairs	12.00
Christmas giving	0

This couple rents an apartment in the Midwest. They make all their own gifts, recycle magazines with friends, freeze food in season, repair their own clothes, and like to walk and watch television. They visit local and area parks and "enjoy driving all over." They retired at fifty-eight and are coping very nicely, thank you, on their $1,317 a month.

Retired Couple No. 4
Monthly Budget: $1,430

Sources of Income:

Social Security	37%
Pension	23%
Investments	40%

Monthly Spending:

Housing	$100.00
Utilities	230.00
Food	250.00
Eating Out	50.00
Church/Charities	100.00
Goods/Services	300.00
Insurance	100.00
Health Care	50.00
Transportation	80.00
Leisure/Recreation/Hobbies	0
Travel/Vacations	100.00
Repairs	29.17
Christmas giving	41.67

This couple lives in Nevada and retired at sixty-two. They love to take day trips, sometimes into Reno or Yosemite Park in California. They own their condominium, so their only housing expense is property tax. They're really involved in the activities at their senior citizen center, and contribute 230 hours a month of volunteer work. Their one desire is to take a cruise.

Retired Couple No. 5
Monthly Budget: $1,504

Sources of Income:

Social Security	29%
Pension	29%
Investments	42%

Monthly Spending:

Housing	$300.00
Utilities	150.00
Food	250.00
Eating Out	60.00
Church/Charities	120.00
Goods/Services	30.00
Insurance	120.00
Health Care	110.00
Transportation	100.00
Leisure/Recreation/Hobbies	150.00

Travel/Vacations	*50.00*
Repairs	*34.00*
Christmas giving	*30.00*

This is one of the couples I interviewed at Sun City Tucson, Arizona. They're deeply involved in all the retirement activities at Sun City, including swimming, walking, square and ballroom dancing. They save money by buying gifts on sale, checking books out of the library (rather than buying them), and she cuts mister's hair. They buy all their food in quantity at the Price Club, and they always combine trips to save transportation costs. They only go to doctors who take Medicare assignment, and they order their prescriptions from a large discount drug company. They retired at fifty-five and took part-time jobs to get by until they started drawing their Social Security benefits at age sixty-five. They're happy they "semi-retired" early.

Retired Couple No. 6
Monthly Budget: $1,574

Sources of Income:

Social Security	*55%*
Pension	*30%*
Investments	*14%*
Part-time jobs	*1%*

Monthly Spending:

Housing	*$230.00*
Utilities	*114.00*
Food	*130.00*
Eating Out	*0*
Church/Charities	*377.00*
Goods/Services	*78.00*
Insurance	*233.00*
Health Care	*110.00*
Transportation	*97.00*

Leisure/Recreation/Hobbies	*31.00*
Travel/Vacations	*108.00*
Repairs	*20.00*
Christmas giving	*46.25*

This couple lives in Bristol Village, Waverly, Ohio. He retired from the ministry at seventy, and she retired from her position as a legal secretary at sixty-five, when they moved to Bristol Village. They have a life lease on a home in this retirement community, which they enjoy so much that they rarely travel. Their lives are centered around church and the activities of the community, "mostly music." They stay healthy by "refraining from smoking and drinking, eating moderately, and walking daily."

Retired Couple No. 7
Monthly Budget: $1,623

Sources of Income:

Social Security	*45%*
Pension	*36%*
Investments	*19%*

Monthly Spending:

Housing	*$250.00*
Utilities	*200.00*
Food	*200.00*
Eating Out	*300.00*
Church/Charities	*50.00*
Goods/Services	*100.00*
Insurance	*100.00*
Health Care	*163.00*
Transportation	*60.00*
Leisure/Recreation/Hobbies	*50.00*
Travel/Vacations	*50.00*
Repairs	*16.70*
Christmas giving	*83.34*

This couple lives in Pine Lakes Country

Club, in North Fort Myers, Florida. They love to eat out, a big part of their monthly spending. They do take advantage of sales and use coupons, too. They have one car and always look for "the cheapest gas." They love to go "visiting" and entertain others in their home. They spend about $50 a month on woodworking and craft supplies. They always go to doctors who accept Medicare assignment, and their only traveling consists of attending free exhibits and shows. Their retirement community has an activities director who keeps the calendar full of "free stuff to do."

Retired Couple No. 8
Monthly Budget: $1,992

Sources of Income:

Social Security	29%
Pension	29%
Investments	42%

Monthly Spending:

Housing (taxes only)	$100.00
Utilities	100.00
Food	250.00
Eating Out	100.00
Church/Charities	200.00
Goods/Services	50.00
Insurance	300.00
Health Care	200.00
Transportation	100.00
Leisure/Recreation/Hobbies	50.00
Travel/Vacations	416.00
Repairs	42.00
Christmas giving	84.00

This Southwest couple owns their home, so they have money left over for traveling, which they enjoy. They avoid compulsive spending on unnecessary

items, and buy clothes only as needed. They've been married forty-five years, and say the key to staying on their budget through the years has been to "keep track of every dollar spent." They, like so many of the retirees I interviewed, believe that prevention is important in keeping health costs down. They never miss their six-month dental checkups and yearly physicals. They take one expensive trip (nearly $10,000) every two years, which accounts for their $416 a month budgeted toward "travel."

Retired Couple No. 9
Monthly Budget: $1,966

Sources of Income:

Social Security	36%
Investments	64%

Monthly Spending:

Housing	$255.00
Utilities	150.00
Food	400.00
Eating Out	60.00
Church/Charities	45.00
Goods/Services	65.00
Insurance	307.00
Health Care	270.00
Transportation	60.00
Leisure/Recreation/Hobbies	220.00
Travel/Vacations	70.00
Repairs	30.00
Christmas giving	34.00

This Florida couple loves to go to the beach and play golf and tennis. They save money by borrowing books from the library, sending cash gifts, and purchasing clothing that doesn't need to be dry-cleaned. He retired at sixty-three and she at fifty-four; they're glad they retired early enough to enjoy themselves.

Retired Couple No. 10
Monthly Budget: $2,023

Sources of Income:

Social Security	27%
Pension	27%
Part-time jobs	46%

Monthly Spending:

Housing	$500.00
Utilities	150.00
Food	250.00
Eating Out	50.00
Church/Charities	10.00
Goods/Services	200.00
Insurance	150.00
Health Care	5.00
Transportation	500.00
Leisure/Recreation/Hobbies	50.00
Travel/Vacations	100.00
Repairs	25.00
Christmas giving	33.00

This couple is buying a mobile home. They always watch for sales and "clothes you can launder." She fixes her own hair, and they both clip coupons. They save money on transportation by combining trips to save on gas and walking whenever they can. They admit to being "conned" once when they agreed to listen to a presentation on condominiums. They were supposed to receive a stereo for their time, but "that turned out to be a farce." Because he was forced to retire at fifty-nine due to a cutback in personnel, they moved to a retirement community where she works as a receptionist. They're typical of those who get caught without adequate investments when they retire, so they supplement their Social Security and pension income with work when they can get it.

Retired Couple No. 11
Monthly Budget: $2,062

Sources of Income:

Social Security	38%
Pension	33%
Investments	3%
Part-time jobs	26%

Monthly Spending:

Housing	$730.00
Utilities	60.00
Food	400.00
Eating Out	100.00
Church/Charities	20.00
Goods/Services	100.00
Insurance	120.00
Health Care	100.00
Transportation	40.00
Leisure/Recreation/Hobbies	108.00
Travel/Vacations	200.00
Repairs	0
Christmas giving	84.00

This couple also lives in Pine Lakes Country Club in North Fort Myers, Florida. He was fifty-six when they retired, and she fifty-three. They say they "have never been sorry" they retired so young. They play golf and swim, and she's an artist, so she spends some of her leisure time painting. They have excellent health insurance that's paid by his former employer. They love to go to museums and visit state parks. She works in marketing, which brings in $202 a week in income. They don't really need the extra money, but she enjoys her part-time job. Their housing costs are high and they spend a lot on food because of visits from family, but they seem to be living very happily within their means.

Retired Couple No. 12
Monthly Budget: $2,318

Sources of Income:

Pension	80%
Investments	20%

Monthly Spending:

Housing	$989.00
Utilities	150.00
Food	200.00
Eating Out	100.00
Church/Charities	50.00
Goods/Services	125.00
Insurance	225.00
Health Care	35.00
Transportation	40.00
Leisure/Recreation/Hobbies	258.00
Travel/Vacations	100.00
Repairs	17.00
Christmas giving	29.00

This couple are retired travel agents; they "just got tired of working and intend to enjoy life." They retired to Sun City Tucson, Arizona, where they live in one of the outstanding homes offered there. They're pretty sick of traveling, so they do very little. They always shop for bargains by using coupons and watching for sales. Their income will increase, of course, when they reach sixty-two or sixty-five and begin collecting their Social Security benefits.

There, you see? Aren't you encouraged? Others are able to live on small retirement budgets, and so can you! I admit that all of those I interviewed are managing their spending very well. There are no sail boats, or binges to Vegas, or expensive new cars. Many of them live in mobile or manufactured homes such as those at Pine Lakes Country Club, but they all seem to have adequate space, even for entertaining. None of their fingers were "dripping with diamonds," and their closets are filled with "wash-and-wear" clothes, but what difference does that make? The *important* things are affordable: decent housing, one car in good running condition, health insurance, healthy foods, and plenty of recreation and leisure activities.

Get your pad of paper out and start figuring! You can make it work, too!

Chapter Fourteen
It's Your Decision!
[Prioritizing Your Retirement Spending]

Choices! Choices! It all depends on choices! You *can* have a happy and rewarding retirement on your available income, depending on the *choices* you make.

Don't feel sorry for yourself if you're not retiring on the "dream income" you always envisioned. Just remember that the best years of your life lie ahead of you! You *can* enjoy them on the income you *do* have — just make wise choices and comfort yourselves with this fact: "Even the rich are miserable if they live beyond their means." Yes, that is the key — to live within your means. The couples mentioned in the last chapter are doing it, and you can too.

If you choose to stay in your high-cost community to be near your children and close friends, you'll need to budget more for housing than those retirees who move to less expensive areas. This choice will determine your life-style and how much money you have left over for other things.

On the other hand, if you choose the vagabond life of an RVer, your housing needs may be minimal, especially if you only plan to use your home as a "truck stop" in between trips.

What kind of life-style do you choose? And how much money will it leave for other things?

This is what I recommend: Take a morning, with a couple pots of coffee, and sit down with a pad of paper. Divide the paper into three sections, labeled like this:

---

1. *Must have.*
2. *Want, if possible.*
3. *Doesn't matter.*

Under the first category, list the top three or four things you really want when you retire. Some things found on this list might be: "to live in the country, away from traffic and noise" or "to play golf all day long" or "to live in a retirement community with lots of activities and built-in friends."

Category two may list things like "own a self-contained camping trailer" or "live within no more than a two-hour drive from our kids" or "be close to a good church."

The third list might have things such as these: "own two cars" or "be close to a senior center" or "live close to shopping."

Fill in your three lists and then sit back, with another mug of coffee, and analyze them. You'll find that by forcing yourselves to make these lists, the prioritizing will be done automatically and your choices will be made.

Let's say that the first thing on the list of musts is "to be able to play unlimited golf on a quality course for under $100 a month." This means you'll need to scout out golf courses you can afford in communities that have reasonable housing and other services for seniors. This is very possible to do, whether the course is part of a retirement community, as we have already discussed, or a public course in a town you can afford.

I'll give you an example of this very thing: Rancho del Rey Golf Club in Atwater, California. It's as beautiful as many private clubs, complete with lakes full of ducks and blue heron, but they only charge $100 a month per couple for all the rounds of golf they want. The community, although not known as a retirement town, is one of those California valley cities that has a relatively low cost of living. This may be the kind of situation you need to find in the area where you live if golf is of number one importance to you.

If your number one desire is to escape the noise and stress of the big city, you can still find those Norman Rockwell communities scattered around the country. These little towns will not only reduce your stress, but will also lower your cost of retirement living.

I talked to a couple the other day, in fact, who are retiring in three months. They feel they can't afford to live on their retirement income in California and have decided to look for a small town in Oregon. They are disgusted with the new tax increases in California due to the state's latest budget crisis. They're sure they can live more reasonably in Oregon and can't wait to find their special spot, perhaps a little Mayberry, complete with its very own Barney and Aunt Bea. One thing they know for sure: Oregon has no sales tax at all, compared to California's new tax of 7.25 percent. Sure, they'll be leaving all their friends and family, and a home they've grown to love. In fact, they don't know anyone in Oregon, but they do know the move will eliminate their financial stress because they'll retire to a lazy, little town they can afford.

If a small town appeals to you, there are thousands to consider. The choice is up to you—you are in control of your future. Make out your own priority list and pursue your "Number Ones."

My husband and I made up our own list recently. At the top of our *Must Have's* were these three things:

---

1. Live within a half day's drive of our family.
2. Live within a two-hour drive of the Pacific Ocean.
3. Live in a retirement community that is upbeat and active, complete with golf and swimming.

Some may wonder why the Pacific Ocean is so high on our list. You see, we live two hours from the ocean now and visit it once a month. As we walk along our favorite beach near Carmel, we can feel our "coping mechanism" being overhauled. I'm sure these little visits save us thousands of dollars in doctor and counselor fees. Being near the ocean makes us both feel peaceful; all anxieties seem to disappear. I'm sure this sounds real corny to some, but corny or not, the ocean is definitely on our list of *Must Have's*.

I'm curious about your list of priorities, but the important thing is to realize that you can have your desired life-style on your available budget, but it may mean a little *flexibility*! Be willing to change your habits, get out of your rut, and even make a move, if necessary, to set yourselves up with the retirement of your choice, *while living within your means*.

You *can* do it!

GOOD LUCK

AND

HAPPY RETIREMENT!

Appendix A

[Where Retirees Can Find Help]

Consumer Advice

American Association of Retired Persons (AARP)
Consumer Affairs, Program Department
1909 K Street, NW
Washington, DC 20049
(202)728-4355 or (800)234-5772

Better Business Bureau
Consumer Information Services
1515 Wilson Blvd.
Arlington, VA 22209

Consumer Information Catalog
Department B
Pueblo, CO 81009

Consumer Product Safety Commission
5401 W. Bard Ave.
Bethesda, MD 20207
(800)638-8270

Consumers Union of the United States
256 Washington St.
Mt. Vernon, NY 10553
(914)667-9400
(Publishes *Consumer Reports.*)

Cooperative Extension Office
(Local office is listed under State, Federal or County Government in your phone directory.)

Federal Trade Commission, Public Reference
6th and Pennsylvania Ave., NW
Washington, DC 20580
(202)326-2222

Ralph Nader
P.O. Box 19367
Washington, DC 20036

Fix-It Hotlines:

General Electric: (800)626-2000
Maytag: (800)688-9900
Whirlpool: (800)253-1301
White/Westinghouse: (800)245-0600

Investment Income Planning

Associations that can recommend financial advisers

Institute for Certified Financial Planners
10065 E. Harvard Ave.
Denver, CO 80231

International Association of Financial Planners
5775 Peachtree-Dunwoody Rd.
Atlanta, GA 30342

Investing

Publications available from AARP:

Modern Maturity: Personal Finances
   Special Issue
What to Do with What You've Got
Take Charge of Your Money
239 Ways to Put Your Money to Work
Money Matters

No-load mutual fund information

Investment Company Institute
1600 M Street, NW
Washington DC 20036
(*Guide to Mutual Funds* — $1.00.)

No-Load Mutual Fund Association
11 Penn Plaza
New York, NY 10001
(Information on mutual funds that do not charge commissions.)

Extra Income

Home businesses

Small Business Association Publications
P.O. Box 30
Denver, CO 80201-0030
(Free directory of publications and video-tapes.)

Part-time employment

Green Thumb, Inc.
1012 14th St., NW
Washington, DC 20005

Mature Temps
Exxon Building
1251 Avenue of the Americas
New York, NY 10020

National Council of Senior Citizens
925 15th St., NW
Washington, DC 20005

Operation ABLE
180 N. Wabash Ave., Ste. 802
Chicago, IL 60601

Senior Career Planning & Placement
   Service
275 Park Ave., S.
New York, NY 10010
(Places retired executives in part-time po-sitions across the country.)

U.S. Small Business Administration (SBA)
1441 L Street, NW
Washington, DC 20549

General Resources

American Association of Retired Persons
(AARP): Contact information is on p.121.

Barter America magazine
777 S. Main St., Ste. 77
Orange, CA 92668
(714)543-8283

International Reciprocal Trade Assn.
5152 Woodmire Lane
Alexandria, VA 22331
(703)931-0105

Mature Outlook
6001 N. Clark St.
Chicago, IL 60660
(800)336-6330

National Council of Senior Citizens
925 15th St., NW
Washington, DC 20005
(202)347-8800

Social Security Administration
6401 Security Blvd.
Baltimore, MD 21235
(800)325-0778
(800)937-2000

Health

American Cancer Society: (800)227-2345

American College of Surgeons
Office of Public Information
55 E. Erie St.
Chicago, IL 60611
(*When You Need an Operation* — free.)

American Diabetes Association
National Service Center
(800)232-3472

American Heart Association:
(800)373-6300

American Physical Fitness Research
  Institute
654 N. Sepulveda Blvd.
Los Angeles, CA 90049
(213)426-6241

Arthritis Foundation: (404)872-7100

Department of Health and Human
  Services
Food and Drug Administration
Office of Public Affairs
5600 Fishers Lane
Rockville, MD 20857
(DHHS Publication No. FDA-90-1080:
Hocus-Pocus as Applied to Arthritis.)

The Drug Emporium
7792 Olentangy River Rd.
Worthington, OH 43085
(614)846-2511

Fifty-Plus Runners Association
P.O. Box D
Stanford, CA 94309
(415)723-9790

Group Health Association of America:
(202)778-3200
(Information on health maintenance
organizations.)

Joint Commission on Accreditation of
  Hospitals (JCAH)
875 N. Michigan Ave.
Chicago, IL 60611
(List of accredited hospitals.)

John Hopkins Hospital
Hearing and Speech Clinic
(301)955-3434
(Free hearing test over the phone.)

National Cancer Institute:
(800)4-CANCER
*Diet, Nutrition and Cancer Prevention:
  The Good News*

National Digestive Diseases Education
  and Information Clearinghouse
Box NDDIC
Bethesda, MD 20892
(General information.)

National Institute of Aging Exercise
Bldg. 31, Room 5C35
Bethesda, MD 20892

National Institute of Allergy and
  Infectious Diseases
Box AP, Bldg. 31, Room 7A32
Bethesda, MD 20892
(*On Flu* — free.)

National Association of Mall Walkers
P.O. Box 191
Hermann, MO 65041
(314)486-3945

National Osteoporosis Foundation:
(202)223-2226

Purina Pets for People
Checkerboard Square, 6T
St. Louis, MO 63164
(314)982-3028

Surgery HHS
Washington, DC 20201)
(*Thinking of Having Surgery?*—free.)

Veterans Health Services
Department of Veterans Affairs
810 Vermont Ave., NW
Washington, DC 20420
(202)233-3975

Housing

Publications available from Consumer
  Housing Information Services for Se-
  niors, AARP:
Home-made Money
Housing Options for Older Americans
Planning Your Retirement Housing
*Sunbelt Retirement: The Complete State-
  by-State Guide to Retiring in the South
  and West*
Retirement Edens Outside the Sunbelt
*Relocation Tax Guide: State Tax Infor-
  mation for Relocation Decisions,*
  D13400 (Available from AARP Fulfill-
  ment—EE175.)

Distribution Center
Cornell University
7 Research Park
Ithaca, NY 14850
(Housing options for seniors.)

Insurance and Taxes

Publications available from AARP:
*More Health for Your Dollar—An Older
  Person's Guide to HMOs*

*Insurance Checklist for Life, Auto, Heath
  and Residential*
Property Tax Relief
Insurance Checklist
*Policy Wise: The Practical Guide to
  Insurance Decisions for Older
  Consumers*
*Relocation Tax Guide: State Tax Infor-
  mation for Relocation Decisions,*
  D13400 (Available from AARP Fulfill-
  ment—EE175.)

U.S. Department of Health and Human
  Services
6325 Security Blvd.
Baltimore, MD 21207
(DHHS Publication No. HCFA-02110:
*Guide to Health Insurance for People
With Medicare*.)

Legal Help

Publications available from AARP:
Elderly Law Manual
Legal Rights Calendar
Public Benefits Checklist

American Bar Association
Commission on Legal Problems of the
  Elderly
1800 M Street, NW
Washington, DC 20036
(202)331-2297

Department of the Interior Legal Support
  Services
18th & C Streets, NW
Washington, DC 20240

Legal Services Department
400 Virginia Ave., SW
Washington, DC 20024
(202)863-1820

National Legal Aid and Defenders
  Association
2100 M Street, NW
Washington, DC 20037

National Senior Citizens Law Center
2025 M Street, NW
Washington, DC 20036
(202)887-5280
or:
1052 W. Sixth St.
Los Angeles, CA 90017
(213)482-3550

Leisure

Becoming a School Partner (Available
from AARP Fulfillment EE083.)

National Association of Partners in Education (NAPE)
601 Wythe St., Ste. 200
Alexandria, VA 22314
(703)836-4880
(Volunteer tutors.)

AARP Volunteer Talent Bank: Contact information is on p.121.

Nutrition

American Institute for Cancer Research
Nutrition Hotline: (800)843-8114

Human Nutrition Information Service
U.S. Department of Agriculture
6505 Belcrest Rd., Room 325-A
Hyattsville, MD 20782
*Thrifty Meals for Two: Making Food Dol-
  lars Count*
Dietary Guidelines for Americans
(Home and Garden Bulletins No. 244 and
No. 232.)

Rodale Books
Box 8
Emmaus, PA 18099-0008
Prevention's Meals that Heal Cookbook
The Doctor's Book of Home Remedies
Prevention magazine

Senior Gardening and Nutrition Project
College of Human Development
University of Oregon
Eugene, OR 97403-1273

U.S. Department of Agriculture Hotline:
(800)535-4555
(For questions on food safety.)

Weight Watchers: (800)726-6108
Healthy Living for Life

Transportation

American Automobile Association (AAA)
Mail Stop 150
1000 AAA Dr.
Heathrow, FL 32746-5063
(800)652-1158
(*Gas Watcher's Guide* — free.)
(Also, car counseling given by phone.)

U.S. Department of Transportation Hotline: (800)424-9393
(To find out which car models have ever
been recalled.)

Consumer Information Center-V
P.O. Box 100
Pueblo, CO 81002
(*New Car Buying Guide* — 50 cents.)

Travel: Getting there

Airlines that offer senior discounts

Alaska Airlines (800)426-0333
Aloha Airlines (800)367-5250

America West (800)247-5692
American Airlines (800)433-7300
Braniff (800)BRANIFF
Continental (800)525-0280
Delta (800)221-1212
Hawaiian Air (800)367-5320
Midway (800)621-5700
Northwest (800)225-2525
Pan Am (800)221-1111
Southwest (800)5315601
TWA (800)221-2000
United (800)628-2868
U.S. Air (800)428-4322

Foreign airlines that offer senior discounts

Air Canada (800)422-6232
Alitalia (800)223-5730
British Airways (800)247-9297
Canadian Airlines (800)426-7000
El Al (800)223-6700
Finnair (800)777-5553
Iberia (800)772-4642
KLM/Royal Dutch Airways (800)777-5553
Lufthansa (800)645-3880
Mexicana (800)531-7921
Sabena (800)632-8050
SAS (800)221-2350
TAP Air Portugal (800)221-7370

Cruises

Cruise Line International Association
500 Fifth Ave.
New York, NY 10110

Car rental agencies that offer senior discounts

Alamo (800)327-9633
Avis (800)331-1800
Budget (800)527-0700

Cruise America (800)327-7778
  (Recreational vehicle rentals.)
Dollar (800)421-6868
Hertz (800)654-3131
National (800)328-4567
Thrifty (800)367-2277

Discount travel clubs

Amoco Multicard
200 E. Randolph Dr.
Chicago, IL 60601

Concierge Card
1050 Yuma St.
Denver, CO 80204

Encore (800)638-8976

Privilege (404)823-0066

Quest International
Box 4041
Yakima, WA 89801

Travel America/Entertainment
  Publications
2125 Butterfield Rd.
Troy, MI 48084

Travel Umlimited (800)521-9640

World Umlimited (714)492-0280

Motor clubs

Amoco (800)334-3300
ALA Auto and Travel Club (617)237-5200
Allstate Motor Club (800)232-6282
Chevron Travel Club (415)827-6000
Exxon Travel Club (713)680-5723
Montgomery Ward Motor Club
  (800)621-5151
National Automobile Club (213)386-6591
Shell Motorist Club Plus (713)241-6161

Texaco Star Club (214)258-2060
United States Auto Club (800)348-2761

Recreational vehicle organizations

Family Motor Coach Association
8291 Clough Pike
Cincinnati, OH 45254
(513)474-3622

Good Sam Club
P.O. Box 500
Agoura, CA 91301
(800)423-5061 or
(800)382-3455 in California

RV Adventure Caravan
% Sierra RV
P.O. Box 18070
Reno, NV 89511

Travel: Staying There

Camping

Superintendent of Documents
U.S. Government Printing Office
Department 33
Washington, DC 20402
(*National Parks: Camping Guide*, #024-005-01038-9 — $3.50. Golden Age Passport — free to anyone 62 or older for free lifetime entrance to all federal government parks. Golden Eagle Passport — under age 62, $25 with same benefits.)

National Park Service
Office of Public Inquiries
P.O. Box 37127
Washington, DC 20013-7127
(General camping information for national parks.)

Parks Canada
Ottawa, Ontario
K1A 1G2, Canada

Trailer Life RV Campground Directory
29901 Agoura Rd.
Agoura, CA 91301
(Private campground directory.)

Wheelers RV Campground Guide
1310 Jarvis
Elk Grove, IL 60007
(Private campground directory.)

Kampgrounds of America (KOA)
550 N. 31st St., 4th Fl.
Billings, MT 59101
(Senior discount card; campground directory — $4.)

Leisure Systems, Inc.
14 S. Third Ave.
Sturgeon Bay, WI 54235
(800)358-9163
(15% discount to Yogi Bear's Jellystone Park Camp Resorts and Safari Campgrounds.)

Campus housing

Campus Travel Service
P.O.Box 5007
Laguna Beach, CA 92652
(714)497-3044

Hotels and motels that offer senior discounts

Allstar Inns (805)687-3383
Best Western (800)528-1234
Budget Host Inns (817)828-7447
Budgetel Inns (800)428-3438
Canadian Pacific (800)828-7447

Clarion (800)252-7466
Colony Hotels (800)777-1700
Comfort Inns (800)228-5150
Compri Hotels (800)426-6774
Country Hearth (800)848-5767
Days Inn (800)325-2525
Doubletree Hotels (800)325-2525
Drury Inns (800)325-8300
Econo-Lodge (800)446-6900
Economy Inns (800)826-0778
Embassy Suites (800)362-2779
Friendship Inns (800)453-4511
Hampton Inns (800)HAMPTON
Harley Hotels (800)321-2323
Hilton Hotels (214)239-0511
Holiday Inns (800)HOLIDAY
Howard Johnsons (800)634-3464
Hyatt Hotels (800)228-9000
Imperial 400 Inns (800)368-4400
Inn Suites (800)842-4242
Knights Inns (614)755-6230
LaQuinta Inns (800)531-5900
L-K & Country Inns (800)228-5711
Marriot (800)228-9290
Nendels Motor Inn (800)547-0106
Omni Hotels (800)843-6664
Quality Inns (800)228-5151
Radisson Hotels (800)228-9822
Ramada Inns (800)2-RAMADA
Red Carpet Inns (800)251-1962
Rodeway Inns (800)228-2000
Sandman Hotels (800)663-6900
Scottish Hotels (800)251-1962
Sheraton Hotels (800)325-3535
Shoney's Inns (800)222-2222
Sonesta Hotels (800)343-7170
Stouffer Hotels (800)HOTELS-1
Travelodge/Viscount (800)255-3050
Treadway Inns (800)631-0182
Vagabond Inns (800)522-1555
Westin Hotels (800)228-3000
Westmark Hotels (800)544-0970

Motels that offer low rates to the general public (some also offer senior discounts)

E-Z 8 Motels (619)291-4284
Motel 6 (214)386-6161
Red Roof Inns (800)843-7663
Regal 8 Inns (800)851-8888
Super 8 Motels (800)843-1991
Susse Chalet (800)258-1980 or
    (800)572-1880 (in New Hampshire)

Hostels

American Youth Hostels
P.O. Box 37613
Washington, DC 20013-7613

Canadian Hostelling Association
333 River Rd.
Vanier, Ontario
K1L 8H9, Canada
($15 senior citizen membership fee.)

To trade houses or apartments

The Evergreen Club
1926 S. Pacific Coast Hwy.
Redondo Beach, CA 90277

Global Home Exchange
Box 2015
South Burlington, VT 05407

Home Exchange International
P.O. Box 878
New York, NY 10038

INNter Lodging Co-op
P.O. Box 7044
Tacoma, WA 98407

International Home Exchange Service
(Intervc US)
P.O. Box 190070
San Francisco, CA 94119

Loan-a-Home
Two Park Lane, Apt. 6E
Mt. Vernon, NY 10552

Teacher Swap
P.O. Box 4130
Rocky Point, NY 11778
(Exclusively for teachers)

Senior Travel Exchange Program (STEP)
P.O. Box H
Santa Maria, CA 93456

Vacation Exchange Club
12006 111th Ave.
Youngtown, AZ 85363

Travel: Thrill/Chill Vacations

Adventure vacations

Carlson Travel Network
P.O. Box 92393
Anchorage, AK 99509-2393

MarkTours
P.O. Box 196769
Anchorage, AK 99519-6769

Mt. Robson Adventure Holidays
P.O. Box 146
Valemount, British Columbia
V0E 2Z0, Canada

National Audubon Society
613 Riversville Rd.
Greenwich, CT 66831

Ocean Voyages
1709 Bridgeway
Sausalito, CA 94965

Overseas Adventure Travel
349 Broadway
Cambridge, MA 02139

Outdoor Vacations for Women Over 40
P.O. Box 200
Groton, MA 01450

Outward Bound USA
384 Field Point Rd.
Greenwich, CT 06830

Over the Hill Gang
13791 E. Rice P.
Aurora, CO 80015

Sierra Club
730 Polk St.
San Francisco, CA 94109

Sobek Expeditions
P.O. Box 1089
Angels Camp, CA 95222

Special Expeditions
720 Fifth Ave., Room 605
New York, NY 10019

Travent
P.O. Box 305
Waterbury Center, VT 05677

The Wilderness Society
1400 Eye St., NW
Washington, DC 20005

Wilderness Travel
801 Allston Way
Berkeley, CA 94710

Archaeologist vacations

Foundation for Field Research
P.O. Box 2010
Alpine, CA 92001
(609)445-9264

Biking tours

American Youth Hostels National Office
P.O. Box 37613
Washington, DC 20013-7613

American Lung Association
(916)444-LUNG

Backroads Bicycle Touring
1516 Fifth St., Ste. H20
Berkeley, CA 94710

Bicycling
33 E. Minor St.
Emmaus, PA 18098
(The largest U.S. monthly bicycling magazine.)

Bikecentennial
P.O. Box 8308-PF
Missoula, MT 59807
(State-by-state list of 140 U.S. bicycle tour operators; 60+ membership — $17/year.)

The Countryman Press, Inc.
P.O. Box 175
Woodstock VT 05091
(Free catalog of U.S. bicycle touring publications.)

Cowboy-for-a-week

Farm & Ranch Vacations, Inc.
36 E. 57th St.
New York, NY 10022
(800)272-8282

Mountain climbing tours

Earthwatch
680 Mount Auburn St.
Watertown, MA 02171

Scuba diving vacations

Atlantis Submarines
31921 Camino Capistrano, Ste. 9-122
San Juan Capistrano, CA 92675

White water rafting

Colorado River White Water Rafting
Department of Boating and Waterways
1629 S Street
Sacramento, CA 95814-7291

National Forest White Water Rafting —
Western states (800)552-3625

World travel

Travel Dynamics
132 E. 70th St.
New York, NY 10021
(800)267-6766

Travel: Going together

Organizations that match travel companions

American Jewish Congress
15 E. 84th St.
New York, NY 10028

Breeze Tours
2750 Sickney Point Rd.
Sarasota, FL 33581

Golden Age Travellers
Pier 27, The Embarcadero
San Francisco, CA 94111

Golden Companions
P.O. Box 754
Pullman, WA 99163

Loners of America
191 Villa Del Rio Blvd.
Boca Raton, FL 33432

Loners on Wheels
808 Lester St.
Poplar Bluff, MO 63901

Mayflower Tours
1225 Warren Ave.
Downers Grove, IL 60515

Merry Widows Dance Cruises
P.O. Box 31087
Tampa, FL 33622

Partners-in-Travel
P.O. Box 491145
Los Angeles, CA 90049

Saga Holidays
120 Boylston St.
Boston, MA 02116

Single World
444 Madison Ave.
New York, NY 10022

Solo Flights
127 S. Compo Rd.
Westport, CT 06880

Suddenly Single Tours
161 Dreiser Loop
New York, NY 10475

Travel Companion Exchange, Inc.
Box 833
Amityville, NY 11701

Tours

Breeze Tours
2750 Stickney Point Rd.
Sarasota, FL 33581

The 50-Plus Club-AJS Travel
177 Beach & 116th Streets
Rockaway Park, NY 11694

Four Winds Travel, Inc.
175 Fifth Ave.
New York, NY 10010

Grand Circle Tours
347 Congress St.
Boston, MA 02210

National Tour Association, Inc.
North American Headquarters
P.O. Box 3071
Lexington, KY 40596-3071

Pleasant Hawaiian Holidays
2404 Townsgate Rd.
Westlake Village, CA 91361

Saga International Tours
Saga International Holidays, Ltd.
120 Boylston St.
Boston, MA 02116

These seniors organizations offer planned tours to their membership

AARP Travel Service
5855 Green Valley Circle
Culver City, CA 90239
(800)227-7737

Disney's Magic Years Club
Box 4709
Anaheim, CA 92803-4709
(714)490-3250

Golden Age Travellers
Pier 27, The Embarcadero
San Francisco, CA 94111
(800)258-8880 or
(800)652-1683 (in California)

Mature Outlook Travel Alert
6001 N. Clark St.
Chicago, IL 60660
(800)336-6330

National Council of Senior Citizens
925 15th St., NW
Washington, DC 20005
(202)347-8800

Travel: Information

General travel information

Anti-Jet Lag Diet
Argonne National Laboratory
9700 S. Cass Ave.
Argonne, IL 60439
(Free copy of diet available for SASE.)

Superintendent of Documents
Pueblo, CO 81009
(*Travel Tips for Older Americans.*)

Bureaus of travel and tourism

Alabama (800)252-2262 or (800)392-8096 (in state)
Alaska (907)465-2012
Arizona (602)542-8687
Arkansas (800)643-8383 or (800)482-8999 (in state)
California (800)862-2543
Colordao (800)433-2656
Connecticut (203)258-4290
Delaware (800)441-8846 or (302)736-4271 (in state)
District of Columbia (202)789-7000
Florida (904)487-1462
Georgia (800)847-4842
Hawaii (808)923-1811
Idaho (800)635-7820
Illinois (800)223-0121 or (312)793-2094 (in state)

Indiana (800)289-6646 or (317)232-8860 (in state)
Iowa (800)345-4692
Kansas (913)296-2009
Kentucky (800)225-8747
Louisiana (800)633-5970
Maine (800)533-9595
Maryland (800)543-1036
Massachusetts (800)447-6277
Michigan (800)543-2937
Minnesota (800)657-3700 or (612)296-5029 (in state)
Mississippi (800)647-2290
Missouri (314)751-1447
Nebraska (800)228-4307 or (800)742-7595 (in state)
Nevada (800)638-2328
New Hampshire (800)238-3608
New Jersey (800)537-7397
New Mexico (800)545-2040
New York (800)225-5697
North Carolina (800)847-4862 or (919)733-4171 (in state)
North Dakota (800)437-2077 or (800)472-2100 (in state)
Ohio (800)282-5393
Oklahoma (800)652-6552
Oregon (800)547-7842 or (800)543-8838 (in state)
Pennsylvania (800)847-4872
Puerto Rico (212)599-6262
Rhode Island (800)556-2484
South Carolina (800)868-2492
South Dakota (800)843-1930
Tennessee (615)741-2158
Texas (800)888-8839
Utah (801)538-1030
Vermont (802)828-3236
Virginia (800)847-4882
Washington (800)544-1800
West Virginia (800)432-8747
Wyoming (800)225-5996

Canadian travel and tourism
The North

Yukon Department of Tourism and
  Information
Bag 2745
Whitehorse, Yukon Territory
Y1A 5B9, Canada

Northwest Territories Tourism
  Information
TravelArctic, Government of Northwest
  Territories
Yellowknife, Northwest Territory
X1A 2L9, Canada

Western Canada

Ministry of Tourism
802-865 Hornby St.
Vancouver, British Columbia
V6Z 2G3, Canada

Alberta Tourism
10155 102nd St.
Edmonston, Alberta
T5J 4L6, Canada

Midwest Canada

Saskatchewan Tourism
1919 Saskatchewan Dr.
Regina, Saskatchewan
S4P 3V7, Canada

Travel Manitoba
155 Carlton St., 7th Fl.
Winnipeg, Manitoga
R3C 3H8, Canada

Ontario/Quebec

Ontario Ministry of Tourism and
  Recreation
77 Bloor St. W.

Toronto, Ontario
M7A 2R9, Canada

Tourism Quebec
800 Victoria Square
Montreal, Quebec
H4Z 1C3, Canada

Atlantic Canada

Tourism New Brunswick
P.O. Box 12345
Fredericton, New Brunswick
E3B 5C3, Canada

Nova Scotia Department of Tourism
P.O. Box 456
Halifax, Nova Scotia
B3J 2R5, Canada

Prince Edward Island Visitor Services
P.O. Box 940
Charlottetown, Prince Edward Island
C1A 7M5, Canada

Travel newsletters with discount information

AARP News Bulletin
1909 K Street, NW
Washington, DC 20049

Mature Outlook Newsletter
6001 N. Clark St.
Chicago, IL 60660-9977

The Mature Traveler
GEM Publishing
P.O. Box 50820
Reno, NV 89513

Appendix B

[Suggested Reading]

Housing

Adler, Joan. *The Retirement Book*, William Morrow & Co., 1975.

Dickinson, Peter A., *Sunbelt Retirement*, E.P. Dutton, 1980.

Savageau, David. *Retirement Places Rated*, Prentice Hall Press, 1990.

Insurance and Taxes

Block, Julian. *Julian Block's Guide to Year-Round Tax Savings*, Homewood, Illinois: Dow Jones-Irwin, 1986.

Breitbard, Stanley H. and Donna Sammons Carpenter. *The Price Waterhouse Book of Personal Financial Planning*, New York: Henry Holt and Co., 1988.

Chasen, Nancy H. *Policy Wise: The Practical Guide to Insurance Decisions for Older Consumers*, Glenview, Ill.: Scott, Foresman and Company, 1983.

Gitman, Lawrence J. and Michael D. Joehnk. *Personal Financial planning*, New York: Henry Holt and Co., 1988.

Heatter, Justin. *Take Charge of Your Finances—and Win Financial Freedom*, New York: Charles Scribner's Sons, 1984.

Kaplan, Lawrence J. *Retiring Right*, Avery, 1990.

Mayer, Thomas R. *Health Insurance Alternative: A Guide to Health Maintenance Organizations*. New York: Putnam Publishing Group, 1984.

Weinstein, Grace W. *The Lifetime Book of Money Management*. New York: New American Library, Inc., 1983.

Leisure Time

Gault, Jan. *Free Time: Making Your Leisure Count*, New York: John Wiley & Sons, Inc., 1983.

Lakein, Alan. *How to Get Control of Your Time and Your Life*. New York: New American Library, 1973.

McCants, Louise. *Retire to Fun and Freedom*, Warner Books, 1990.

Life-styles

Howells, John. *Retirement Choices*, Gateway Books, 1987.

Michaels, Joseph. *Prime of Your Life: A Practical Guide to Your Mature Years*, Boston, Mass: Little, Brown & Co., 1983.

Morrison, Morie. *Retirement in the West*, Chronicle Books, 1976.

Myers, Albet and Christopher P. Andersen. *Success Over Sixty*, New York: Summit Press, 1984.

Making Ends Meet

Applegath, John. *Working Free*, New York: Executive Books, 1982.

Bolles, Ricahrd Nelson, *What Color is Your Parachute?* Berkeley, CA, Ten Speed Press, 1975.

Boroson, Warren. *Keys to Retirement Planning*. Barron's, 1990.

Chidakel, Susan. *Starting and Operating a Playgroup for Profit*. Pilot Books.

Directory of Franchising Organizations Pilot Books.

Editors of Entrepreneur Magazine, *Entrepreneur Magazine's Complete Guide to Owning a Home-Based Business*. Bantam, 1990.

Elgin, Duane. *Volutnary Simplicity*. New York: Morrow, 1981.

Ellis, Iris. *Fabulous Finds: The Sophisticated Shopper's Guide to Factory Outlet Centers*. Writer's Digest Books, 1991.

Federal Reserve System, Board of Governors. *Consumer Handbook to Credit Protection Laws*. Washington, D.C.: 1982.

Givens, Charles J. *Wealth Without Risk*. Simon & Schuster, 1991.

Harmon, Charlotte. *The Flea Market Entrepreneur*. Pilot Books.

Hitchcock, Peggy. *The Garage Sale Handbook*. Pilot Books.

Institute of Lifetime Learning. *Second Career Opportunities for Older Persons*. A service of NRTA and AARP. Washington, D.C.: 1982.

Lester, Mary. *A Woman's Guide to Starting a Small Business*. Pilot Books.

Liebers, Arthur. *How to Start a Profitable Retirement Business*. Pilot Books.

Meaney, James. *Evaluating and Buying a Franchise*. Pilot Books.

Murray, Jean Wilson. *Starting and Operating a Word Processing Service*. Pilot Books.

Null, Gary. *How to Turn Your Ideas Into Dollars*. Pilot Books.

Null, Gary. *Profitable Part-Time, Home Based Businesses*. Pilot Books.

Ruhe-Schoen, Janet. *Organizing and Operating Profitable Workshop Classes*. Pilot Books.

Small, Samuel. *Starting a Business After 50*. Pilot Books.

Smith, Wesley J. *The Senior Citizens' Handbook*. Price Stern Sloan, 1989.

Temple, Mary. *How to Start a Secretarial and Business Service*. Pilot Books.

Whitis, Rose Freeman. *Starting and Operating a Vintage Clothing Shop*. Pilot Books.

Medical

AARP. *Information on Medicare and*

Health Insurance for Older People. Long Beach, Calif.: 1983.

Griffith, H. Winter, M.D. *Complete Guide to Prescription and Non-Prescription Drugs*

Hansen, Leonard J. *Life Begins at 50*. Barron's, 1989.

Prevention Magazine Health Books. *The Doctor's Book of Home Remedies*. Rodale Books, Emmaus, PA.

U.S. Department of Health and Human Services. *Your Medicare Handbook*. Washington, D.C.: U.S. Government Printing Office, 1989.

Nutrition

Dickinson, Peter A. *The Complete Retirement Planning Book*. E.P. Dutton, 1976.

Ways, Peter, M.D. *Take Charge of Your Health*, Lexington, Mass.: The Stephen Greene Press, 1985.

Transportation

Hunnisett, Henry S. *Retirement Guide*, Self-counsel Press, 1990.

Stevenson, Chris Harold. *Auto Repair Shams and Scams*.

Travel

Allstate Motor Club National Park Guide. Prentice-Hall Travel.

Carlson, Ray. *Directory of Free Vacation and Travel Information*. Pilot Books.

Carlson, Ray. *Directory of Low-Cost Vacations with a Difference*. Pilot Books.

Carlson, Raymond. *National Directory of Budget Motels*. Pilot Books.

Carlson, Ray and Maiorino, Maria. *National Directory of Free Tourist Attractions*. Pilot Books.

Dickinson, Peter A. *Travel and Retirement Edens Abroad*. AARP, 1989.

Frommer, Arthur. *Europe on $25 a Day*. Frommer, 1989.

Gluck, Harold. *Avoiding Travel Rip-Offs and Other Tips for Travelers*. Pilot Books.

Heilman, Joan Rattner. *Unbelievably Good Deals and Great Adventures that You Absolutely Can't Get Unless You're Over 50*. Contemporary Books, 1989.

Palmer, Paige. *Guide to the Best Buys in Package Tours*. Pilot Books.

Palmer, Paige. *The Senior Citizen's Guide to Budget Travel in the United States and Canada*. Pilot Books.

Palmer, Paige. *The Travel & Vacation Discount Guide*. Pilot Books.

Philcox and Boe. *How You Can Travel Free as a Group Tour Organizer*. Pilot Books.

Philcox and Boe. *Toll-Free Travel & Vacation Information Directory*. Pilot Books.

Van Meer, Mary and Pasquarelli, Michael Anthony. *Free Attractions, U.S.A.*

To the Reader

I will be updating this book constantly, and I could use your help. Please send me your unique cost-cutting ideas. I would also love to know which of the suggestions in this book have worked in your retirement situation. Write me:

Diane Warner
% Writer's Digest Books
1507 Dana Avenue
Cincinnati, Ohio 45207

Index

OTHER BOOKS OF INTEREST

NEW!
FABULOUS FINDS: A Sophisticated Shopper's Guide to Factory Outlet Centers
Who doesn't want to save money on brand-name items? You can—everyday of the year—with this comprehensive directory of hundreds of factory outlets across the country. Thoroughly researched, Fabulous Finds provides comprehensive information on each outlet listing, including brands and savings available, detailed directions and map illustrations, interesting side trips near the center, plus unique restaurants and lodgings that are located nearby. $12.95/#10242/368 pages/paperback

NEW!
STREAMLINING YOUR LIFE: A 5-Point Plan for Uncomplicated Living
"If I only had the time!" Who hasn't uttered that to himself? With the help of this new book, you'll discover the secrets of a simpler life with time for yourself, your family and your friends. It's filled with specific easy-to-follow steps to help keep life manageable and meaningful, in addition to dozens of tips and techniques for simplified shopping, hassle-free holidays and no-work parties. $11.95/#10238/144 pages/paperback

CONQUERING THE PAPER PILE-UP
If you're inundated with paper—mail, insurance forms, bills, correspondence, business records—this is the book for you! Author Stephanie Culp combines a humorous, you-can-do-it attitude with practical, step-by-step guidelines to help you decide what to toss and what to keep, and how to process, store—and even find again!—every piece of paper in your home or office. $11.95/#10178/176 pages/paperback

HOW TO CONQUER CLUTTER
Conquering clutter is an on-going process. Even after you've heroically cleared it all away, it manages to creep back into your life. Think of this book as a "first aid guide" for when you wake up to find that clutter once again has overtaken every inch of available space. The handy A-to-Z format provides clutter-buster advice for everything in your home. $10.95/#10119/176 pages/paperback

IT'S HERE . . . SOMEWHERE (Revised & Updated)
Tired of those organizational binges where you shuffle stuff from one room to another—and just end up with a neater mess? It's Here . . . Somewhere shows you the secrets of putting your home in order and keeping it that way! This unique system not only keeps your house in order, but can increase storage space, make cleaning easier, and give you long-lasting peace of mind. $10.95/#10214/175 pages/paperback

---

YES! Please send me:

_____ #10242 **Fabulous Finds: A Sophisticated Shopper's Guide to Factory Outlet Centers**

_____ #10238 **Streamlining Your Life: A 5-Point Plan for Uncomplicated Living**

_____ #10178 **Conquering the Paper Pile-Up**

_____ #10119 **How to Conquer Clutter**

_____ #10214 **It's Here . . . Somewhere**

Credit card orders
call toll-free 1-800-289-0963

☐ Payment enclosed

☐ Please charge my: ☐ Visa   ☐ MasterCard

Acct.# _____ Exp.Date _____

Signature _____

Name _____

Address _____

City _____ State _____ Zip _____

Prices subject to change without notice.

Send to: Writer's Digest Books
1507 Dana Avenue
Cincinnati, Ohio 45207

6248